Maple® V Fligl Release

Tutorials for Calculus, Linear Algebra, and Differential Equations

Brooks/Cole Symbolic Computation Series

Maple®
Bauldry/Fiedler, *Calculus Projects with Maple, Second Edition*
Blachman/Mossinghoff, *Maple V Quick Reference*
Belmonte et al., *Solving ODEs with Maple V* (forthcoming)
Boggess et al., *CalcLabs with Maple*
Devitt, *Calculus with Maple V*
Ellis/Johnson/Lodi/Schwalbe, *Maple V Flight Manual, Release 4*
Ellis/Johnson/Lodi/Schwalbe, *Maple V Flight Manual, Release 2 & 3*
Fattahi, *Maple V Calculus Labs, Second Edition*
Johnson, *Linear Algebra with Maple V*

For Macintosh® and Windows® operating systems:
Waterloo Maple Inc., Maple V Release 4 Student Edition
Waterloo Maple Inc., Maple V Release 3 Student Edition

Math T/L
Small/Child, *Exploring Calculus with Math T/L*

For Macintosh operating systems:
Child, Math T/L

Scientific WorkPlace™
Hardy/Walker, *Doing Mathematics with Scientific WorkPlace, Revised Edition*

For Macintosh and Windows operating systems:
TCI Software Research, Scientific WorkPlace, Version 2.5, Student Edition

Mathematica®
Blachman, Boggess et al., *CalcLabs with Mathematica*
Ellis/Lodi, *A Tutorial Introduction to Mathematica*
Johnson, *Linear Algebra with Mathematica*

Maple® V Flight Manual
Release 4
Tutorials for Calculus, Linear Algebra, and Differential Equations

Wade Ellis, Jr.

Eugene Johnson

Ed Lodi

Daniel Schwalbe

Brooks/Cole Publishing Company

I(T)P® An International Thomson Publishing Company

Pacific Grove • Albany • Bonn • Boston • Cincinnati • Detroit
London • Madrid • Melbourne • Mexico City • New York • Paris
San Francisco • Singapore • Tokyo • Toronto • Washington

Sponsoring Editor: *Cynthia Sanner*
Marketing Team: *Carolyn Crockett and Christine Davis*
Editorial Assistant: *Tami McBroom*
Production Coordinator: *Marlene Thom*

Manuscript Editor: *Carol Dondrea*
Cover Design: *Laurie Albrecht*
Typesetting: *Integre Technical Publishing Co., Inc.*
Printing and Binding: *Courier*

For more information, contact:

BROOKS/COLE PUBLISHING COMPANY
511 Forest Lodge Road
Pacific Grove, CA 93950
USA

International Thomson Editores
Seneca 53
Col. Polanco
11560 México D.F., México

International Thomson Publishing Europe
Berkshire House 168–173
High Holborn
London WC1V 7AA
England

International Thomson Publishing GmbH
Königswinterer Strasse 418
53227 Bonn
Germany

Thomas Nelson Australia
102 Dodds Street
South Melbourne, 3205
Victoria, Australia

International Thomson Publishing Asia
221 Henderson Road
#05–10 Henderson Building
Singapore 0315

Nelson Canada
1120 Birchmount Road
Scarborough, Ontario
Canada M1K 5G4

International Thomson Publishing Japan
Hirakawacho Kyowa Building, 3F
2-2-1 Hirakawacho
Chiyoda-ku, Tokyo 102
Japan

Printed in the United States of America

10   9   8   7   6   5   4   3   2

ISBN 0-534-26202-3

Contents

4   Linear Algebra   62

5   Differential Equations   105

Index   161

Preface

This book updates the *Maple® V Flight Manual* for use with *Maple V Release 4*, the latest version of Maple. It includes revisions that incorporate Maple's major new software enhancements and commands. The differential equations chapter has been completely revised to reflect the extensive changes in the differential equations' commands, and the expanded graphical user interface markedly improves the user friendliness of Maple.

The first three chapters are primarily the work of Ed Lodi and Wade Ellis, Jr., although the two other authors made many contributions to these chapters as well. The fourth chapter, on linear algebra, is the work of Eugene Johnson. His efforts also include extensive consultation with the Waterloo Maple Software Group (WMSG) in extending the Maple **linalg** package. Dan Schwalbe created and revised the fifth chapter, on differential equations, in consultation with WMSG and with a great deal of editing help from his wife, Kathryn Schwalbe.

The authors of this book have greatly enjoyed working together over a number of years on this project. The sharing of ideas about computer algebra systems and how to use them in doing, learning, and teaching mathematics has been immensely rewarding. We only hope that the reader will enjoy this work as much as we, the authors, enjoyed the labor of creating it.

Acknowledgments

We would like to express our thanks to the following people from Brooks/Cole Publishing Company: Jeremy Hayhurst, Robert Evans, and Cynthia Sanner for their ongoing efforts toward making

Maple accessible to students in mathematics courses and for bringing the authors together on this project; Marlene Thom, Nancy Conti, and Tami McBroom for their helpfulness and good cheer throughout the production of this book; the design and production staffs, especially Vernon Boes and Laurie Albrecht, for their many helpful suggestions. We are pleased to have worked with the outstanding staff at Brooks/Cole Publishing Company.

We would like to thank the Waterloo Maple Software Group for expanding and refining the Maple V version of the **linalg** package so that it would be more powerful and easier to use. We especially thank WMSG's Mike Monagan, who was the principal programmer for the **linalg** package. The many exchanges of ideas and code with Mike enhanced Maple's **linalg** package, the **ODE2** package, and the chapters on linear algebra and differential equations.

Thanks go to Keith Geddes for initiating and supporting the decision to modify Maple V so that it would be more useful in an instructional environment. We thank Benton Leong for facilitating the timely approval and implementation of software changes. Others in the Waterloo group have also been helpful in testing and making suggestions.

We also thank students in the University of Waterloo Symbolic Computation Group, especially Blair Madore, Lee Qiao, and Katy Simonsen.

Many thanks also go to Jerry Kazdan of the University of Pennsylvania and David Royster of the University of North Carolina for their insightful comments. In addition, we thank William C. Bauldry of Appalachian State University, Maurino P. Bautista of Rochester Institute of Technology, Sharad Keny of Whittier College, Glenn Sowell of the University of Nebraska at Omaha, and Jeanette R. Palmiter of Portland State University for reviewing the previous edition manuscript and for their many suggestions for improving the book. Of course, any errors that remain are our own.

Finally, we would like to thank our wives—Jane, Sandy, Rose, and Kathryn—for their patience, support, and encouragement during the writing and production of this book.

Wade Ellis, Jr.
Eugene W. Johnson
Ed Lodi
Daniel Schwalbe

Introduction

What Are Computer Algebra Systems?

You have learned to solve equations and explore functions in mathematics courses you have taken. The sophisticated manipulation of symbols and expressions that you use to solve equations and investigate functions can also be performed by software packages called *computer algebra systems*. You can use computer algebra systems to generate the exact symbolic solutions you determined by hand, the numerical approximations you found with a calculator, and the graphs you have drawn. As with paper-and-pencil methods of solution and finding graphs, however, the success of computer methods is limited by available time, space, and ability.

The Origins of Computer Algebra Systems

In 1959 at the Massachusetts Institute of Technology, a group of researchers began the development of MACSYMA, a computer algebra system. This first system was the outgrowth of an attempt to convince the science community that computers could perform significant intellectual tasks. Mathematics was chosen as the vehicle for demonstrating the intellectual possibilities of machines because some important and difficult mathematical processes are rule-based, highly structured, and, thus, possibly programmable on a computer. MACSYMA's early successes proved that the computer programming of manipulative mathematics (such as the solving of many elementary differential equations) is not nearly as difficult as one might assume given how hard it seems to be to teach these procedures to people.

The Origins of Maple

In 1980 a group of professors and researchers at the University of Waterloo in Canada began discussions of computer algebra systems and their use in engineering and various fields of mathematics. They decided that the currently available systems were not appropriate tools for the needs of their university, with its strong engineering and mathematics departments, where both research and teaching are important. The Symbolic Computation Group was formed and decided to develop a new computer algebra system that would satisfy several criteria: (1) It should allow many users (including students) to access the system at the same time with minimal computer processing power or memory; (2) it should have a clearly logical and understandable syntax; and (3) it should allow for additional features to be added easily. The outcome of this effort was called Maple.

Maple has been extended and enhanced many times, especially in the last five years. *Maple V Release 4*, the current version, for which this book is written, provides an enhanced graphic user interface that is consistent over a wide variety of computer platforms. Many new commands and functions, especially in differential equations, have been added as well in this new release. *Maple V Release 4* also allows for easier function definition and performs many computations faster than previous releases. This new implementation includes improved speed in two-dimensional graphing, and (on appropriate hardware) color graphics capabilities and more flexible text formatting.

How to Use This Book

You will obtain the greatest benefit from this book by thoughtfully working through each item. Consider carefully the commands you are asked to enter and think about the expected result before you enter the command. Occasionally, in the early chapters of the book, you will be asked to enter commands that will give rise to error messages. This is to provide experience with such errors and to encourage you to experiment fearlessly with Maple commands.

A Note to Users of Mathematics

Maple V is a powerful mathematical tool that has already found significant uses in investigating and analyzing problems in the natural and managerial sciences and in engineering. The symbolic, numeric, and graphical power that Maple V provides can greatly assist you in the mathematical aspects of your work. This book quickly familiarizes you with the Maple V environment and some of the many ways of using Maple to solve problems involving calculus, linear algebra, and differential equations.

Introduction for Instructors

Computer Algebra and the Mathematics Curriculum The mathematics curriculum can be enriched through the intelligent use of computer algebra systems, but this enrichment is not without cost. There will be some trade-offs. Courses will change to reflect the new technology, which will result in a new arrangement of course priorities. Instructors will need to spend more time in teaching these enriched and modified courses. Such new courses should be more interesting, exciting, and challenging for both students and faculty, however. Students with access to a computer algebra system will be able to devote more time to concepts and applications. They can actually experiment with mathematics in a way that was highly impractical before. Thus, computer algebra allows students to sharpen high-level, problem-solving skills while relying on the computer to handle the more mundane details.

The Purpose of the Book

The first three chapters of this book are based on material from precalculus and calculus and are intended as an introduction to the use of computer algebra systems in mathematics and mathematics courses. Although the first three chapters can be used as a supplement to standard calculus courses, a more thorough integration of computer algebra into such courses can best be achieved with materials from books such as Brooks/Cole's *CalcLabs with Maple® V* or *Calculus Projects with Maple® V*.

Chapter 4 provides an outline for a theoretical first course in linear algebra that assumes that any extended computation will be performed using a computer algebra system. Chapter 5 provides an outline for a differential equations course that hinges on computer-based graphical methods and symbol manipulation. Most differential equations are investigated from a graphical and numerical point of view because such equations most often do not possess closed-form solutions. The first three chapters, including a brief introduction to Maple V programming, provide the necessary foundation for the mathematical work in the last two chapters.

The Structure of the Book

This book, as indicated, is constructed around the standard course content of the first two years of college mathematics, including the calculus of one and two variables, linear algebra, and differential equations. The first two chapters introduce well-understood pre-calculus topics as "test" data for mathematical experiments and investigations with the various Maple commands or operators. Once the reader is familiar with Maple's command structure, help facilities, and error recovery methods, the Maple calculus functions are introduced. Techniques for using sets of Maple functions to attack mathematical problems are presented in Chapter 3. The presentation of two-variable calculus topics in this book assumes greater sophistication of the reader; and, therefore, the tutorial features of the book occur less frequently. There is a brief introduction to the automation of sets of commands (also known as programs) at the end of this chapter.

The first three chapters are an introduction to the use of Maple V as a supplement to the standard techniques of paper-and-pencil computation learned in calculus. Though other approaches to this material are possible because of the flexibility of computer algebra systems, we have tried a minimalist approach in these introductory chapters, giving only a brief discussion of programming and requiring none.

In Chapter 4, on linear algebra, Maple is used from the outset to restructure the standard topics from a conceptual point of view rather than a computational one. This chapter is not a textbook for a linear algebra course, but it does provide the necessary computational techniques and rationale for the use of computer algebra systems as an integral part of an introductory linear algebra course. Involved or lengthy computations are done from the beginning with Maple rather than with paper-and-pencil methods, thus allowing greater time to develop and illuminate the conceptual framework behind the computations. Readers who have previously taken courses that use the first part of this book will feel comfortable in working through this chapter even though the presentation has fewer tutorial aspects. Once again, an ever-increasing sophistication in mathematical thinking and computer use is assumed and expected of the reader. The reader is often asked to enter several

Maple commands at once and to reflect more deeply on the results computed by Maple.

In Chapter 5, a new tone and direction for the study of elementary differential equations is developed based on the complete array of tools found in Maple. The graphical, numerical, and symbolic capabilities of Maple are used to lay the groundwork for a course in which modeling is the central theme. The power of Maple allows one to experiment with and become familiar with more interesting examples that motivate the study of the underlying mathematics. Getting an answer is no longer sufficient—understanding the model is the goal.

Readers will gain a more accurate view of the usefulness and beauty of differential equations by understanding more about the nature of solutions rather than just by concentrating on the paper-and-pencil computational skills needed to solve specific types of elementary differential equations. Though this chapter is not a textbook on differential equations, it points the way toward a new, more relevant and interesting course. This new course is more demanding, but also more stimulating and rewarding.

Ways This Book Can Be Used

This book can be used as a computer supplement to any of the courses in the first two years of college. The introductory tutorial material on precalculus mathematics develops the understanding of Maple necessary for its further use in calculus, linear algebra, or differential equations. Individuals who are using technology for the first time in teaching these courses may wish to begin with small technological enhancements. This book will help such teachers make incremental changes to courses while preparing themselves to make more substantial changes based on the instructional and intellectual mastery of a computer algebra system.

Because of its structure and varied emphasis, entire mathematics departments can use this book to gradually, but effectively, introduce computer algebra systems into their course offerings. The tutorial nature of the first chapters allows students and professors alike to become conversant with a computer algebra system without greatly overhauling the traditional courses. Once students and professors are aware of what computer algebra systems can and cannot do, then using them to perform computations in a linear algebra course becomes a simple extension of well-developed ideas about computer computations. Finally, with a sophisticated concept of how and when to use computer algebra systems most fruitfully, a completely revamped differential equations course becomes a natural outgrowth of the use of such a system. With an altered vision of the true nature of the differential equations course, professors will be more able to restructure the elementary calculus courses, through the appropriate use of computer algebra systems, to better develop mathematical maturity in their students.

Courses intended for the mathematical preparation of teachers can use this book as a supplement on computer usage for schools. The wide variety of mathematical content that can be addressed from the Maple package will give the prospective teacher a firm grounding in the possibilities of computer usage in teaching mathematics and the need for their students to become familiar with the uses and possible abuses of technology.

This book can also be used in computer courses intended for engineers and scientists with titles such as Introduction to Computing for Engineers and Scientists. Though these courses are now often taught using the numerical capabilities of Fortran or Pascal, the future engineering and scientific use of computers will surely involve computer algebra systems. This book can be used either as a supplement or as the textbook for such a course.

CHAPTER ONE
Getting Started

The following directions assume a graphical user interface, which will be referred to as a Windows environment. Turn on your computer, enter your Windows environment. Use the mouse to open the Maple folder (if necessary) and the Maple application. Your screen should look something like this:

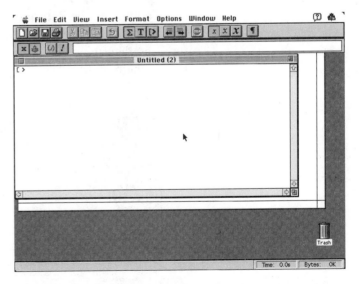

This displayed startup window is called a Maple worksheet. The **>** is the normal Maple prompt, inviting you to enter a Maple command. The icons and menu items at the top of this window allow you to conveniently access some of the most frequently used features of the Maple environment.

Maple and Mathematics

You can easily learn to use the powerful capabilities of Maple if you work through the following tutorial carefully and thoughtfully. It is important, therefore, for you to enter each of the Maple statements that appear in color in the text area. The sentences in the margin on the left describe these commands. Additional explanation follows the Maple commands that appear in color.

You can maximize your understanding if you think carefully about each of the Maple commands and its explanation rather than just entering each in a mechanical fashion. The intent of this presentation is to give you a feel for the interaction that occurs between you, your computer, and Maple. After you are comfortable working with your computer environment and Maple, you will work through examples that will help you learn how to investigate mathematical problems and concepts using Maple.

Using the Help Feature

Use ? to get help at any time in your worksheet.

After you type the **?** symbol, press the key marked Enter on Windows computers or Return on Macintosh and UNIX computers. This book will use "press Enter" to mean "press Enter or Return" as determined by your environment. Your screen should look something like this:

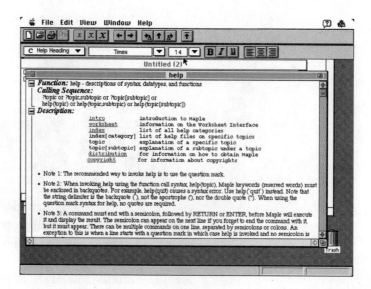

This is a general Help window that describes how to get help on various topics. The Notes provide additional information and explanation. For example, Note 1 indicates that the recommended way to invoke help is to use the question mark (**?**).

You can access the under-lined topics in the Help window.

Click on **intro**
The **intro** Help window appears. You should read this Help window carefully to become familiar with some of Maple's features. You can click on any underlined word to get additional information about it.

You can use the Help facility to find and learn how to use Maple commands. You are encouraged to use it often.

To return to the Maple worksheet, first click on the box in the upper left corner of the **intro** Help window (use the left mouse button on most Windows and UNIX computers). (In the PC and UNIX Windows environments, you can mistakenly use the Close box for the entire Windows environment, in which case you will be asked if you want to exit Windows. You should cancel this operation and use the appropriate Close box.) In the PC Windows environment, select Close from the File popdown menu or use the key combination (Alt-F4) displayed in the Maple environment Close popdown menu. Close the Help window by repeating this operation on its window.

Learning to Use Maple

You can add two numbers.

2 + 3;
Notice the semicolon (**;**) at the end of the line. It is used as a terminator for each statement in Maple. After you have typed the semicolon, you should press Enter. (Remember to press Return on some UNIX workstations.) The answer 5 appears in the middle of the screen followed by the Maple prompt.

You can also add fractions.

2/3 + 1/7;
The fractions are typed with a division sign (**/**). After you type the semicolon (**;**), you should press Enter. Notice that the answer, $\frac{17}{21}$, is displayed in the center of the screen (with a fraction bar and the 17 directly above the 21).

A number can be raised to a power.

2^5;
Your screen should look something like this:

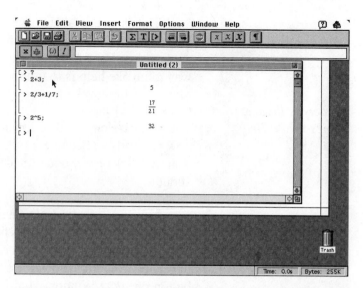

The caret (^) indicates exponentiation. You have asked Maple to find 2^5. As you know, this is 32. This matches the computer output. To validate your typing and Maple's calculations, it is a good idea to think about what the output will be before you execute a command.

What happens when you forget to type the semicolon (;) before you press Enter?

```
2 + 3
```

To simulate this error, be sure *not* to type the semicolon (;) before you press Enter. After you press Enter, a warning is displayed on the screen. You need to decide what is wrong with your statement and fix the problem. In this case, the semicolon is missing.

You can correct this problem.

```
;
```

Type a semicolon and press Enter. The answer 5 appears in the center of the screen when you do this. The Maple prompt appears, inviting you to enter another statement. You can also use the prompt icon ([>) on the Tool bar to obtain the > prompt should you lose it.

Numbers: Integers, Rationals, Decimals

You can also raise 2 to large powers.

```
2^32;
```

Notice that the answer is displayed exactly. This result is different (and correctly so) from what you would obtain on most calculators.

You can raise rational numbers to large powers as well.

```
(2/5)^32;
```

The parentheses are required to ensure that the entire fraction is raised to the 32nd power, not just the denominator. The fraction displayed is once again the exact answer.

A different result occurs if you use another representation of two-fifths.

```
0.4^32;
```

Notice that the displayed answer differs from the previous answer. How many digits are displayed? This answer is similar to what you would expect from a calculator and is the best 10-digit approximation to the exact answer.

*You can force the exact rational answer to be approximated by a decimal using the Maple **evalf** command.*

```
evalf((2/5)^32);
```

Take careful note of the parentheses. The outermost parentheses enclose the argument of the Maple command **evalf**. This result matches the result for the previous statement. It also has 10 digits.

Mistakes often occur when you are entering expressions that have many parentheses in them.

```
evalf(2/5)^32);
```

Be sure to enter the parentheses exactly as shown. The message displayed is a standard message that occurs when Maple does not understand what you entered. Here, there are more right parentheses than left parentheses. You should check for an incorrectly formed statement or a misspelled word whenever a syntax error message occurs. The blinking cursor is placed where Maple runs into the problem. You can either retype the statement or use the editing features of your computer to execute the desired statement. Click on the **[>** button to obtain a new prompt.

You can specify the number of digits that will be displayed in decimal representations of numbers.

```
Digits := 20;
```

You must type a capital **D** in **Digits** because Maple differentiates uppercase and lowercase letters in names. The **:=** symbol (with no space between the **:** and **=**) instructs Maple to assign the value on the right to the variable on the left. This increases the number of digits displayed from the standard 10 to 20. You see that the variable *Digits* is now 20 by the displayed result:

```
Digits := 20
```

Let's look at the decimal representation of 2^{100}.

```
evalf(2^100);
```

Here the result is displayed in 20-digit decimal format. This is also called floating-point format.

You can vary the number of digits in a particular floating-point evaluation.

```
evalf(2^100, 30);
```

Notice that the answer now has 30 digits even though *Digits* is set to 20. Type **Digits := 10;** to reset *Digits* back to 10.

Variables

You can assign a value to a variable.

```
z := 5;
```

This statement assigns the value 5 to the variable *z*. In previous interactions with Maple, you saw an answer. Here, Maple echoes the statement you entered (without the ending semicolon). Maple echoes the statement you enter when no operation is performed that results in an answer.

Maple can evaluate expressions.

```
z^2;
```
The variable z has the value 5. Maple assigns z this value and then evaluates the expression.

Multiplication must be explicitly indicated in the expression to be evaluated.

```
2*z;
```
Multiplication is indicated by an asterisk (*****). The value of the expression when z is 5 is clearly 10.

What happens if you forget an asterisk (*)?

```
2z;
```
The syntax error message indicates that there is a problem with the statement as entered. You have to determine what correction(s) must be made. You would need to reenter the statement (or correct it) with the missing multiplication symbol correctly placed. Type an asterisk (*****) and press Enter.

Reestablish z as a variable with no value assigned to it.

```
z := 'z';
```
The **'** symbol is on the same key with the quote (**"**) symbol.

Check that z has no assigned value.

```
z^2 + 4*z;
```
The expression you entered is displayed in a different way. Notice that z squared is displayed in standard mathematical notation. Also, there is no asterisk in the displayed expression. Although you *must* enter expressions with the exponentiation and multiplication symbols, Maple displays expressions without them.

*The **"** symbol is assigned the value of the last expression evaluated.*

```
";
```
The expression $z^2 + 4z$ is displayed in Maple format.

*You can use the **"** in expressions.*

```
" - 2*z;
```
Maple combines like terms when possible, as you can see.

You can change the expression with other algebraic operations.

```
" - 3;
```
Here, the -3 is simply appended to the expression. Of course, this means that 3 is subtracted from the expression $z^2 + 2z$.

*There is a **factor** command in Maple.*

```
factor(");
```
The factors of the expression assigned to the **"** symbol are displayed.

Check this result using the **expand** *command.*

```
expand(");
```

Always check your results. You may have made a mistake in entering the expression. On rare occasions, Maple makes errors, as most large and complex programs do. These rare errors do not lessen the usefulness of such programs. Develop the habit of checking your Maple computations in the same way you check your hand computations.

An expression can be assigned to a variable name.

```
p := x^2 + 2*x - 3;
```

Note that p is assigned the value $x^2 + 2x - 3$.

You can always check what value is assigned to a variable.

```
p;
```

The value displayed is the value of p.

You can factor the expression p.

```
factor(p);
```

You should check to see that the factors of p are the same as the factors of $x^2 + 2x - 3$ given earlier.

Has factoring p changed p?

```
p;
```

The variable p has remained the same.

Solve the equation $x^2 + 2x - 3 = 0$ *or* $p = 0$.

```
solve(p = 0);
```

The solution is a set of two integers. These integers, as you know, are the solutions to the two equations $(x + 3) = 0$ and $(x - 1) = 0$.

You can plot or graph an expression. You usually need to indicate the interval of the x-values.

```
plot(p, x = -4..4);
```

Notice how the interval of the x-values is specified. You *must* use the two periods rather than a comma. The graph will be displayed after a short time. Your screen should look something like this:

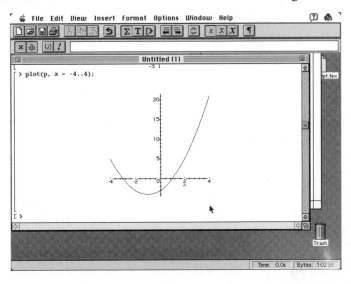

Does the graph intersect the *x*-axis at the same values you obtained solving the equation $p = 0$? You can check this by moving to the left point of the intersection on the *x*-axis and click the mouse button. The horizontal coordinate displayed in the left part of the Tool bar should be close to -3. To enter new commands, move the cursor to the right of the last **[>** and click the mouse button. You are again ready to enter Maple commands.

You can, if you wish, specify the range values.

```
plot(p, x = -4..4, y = -10..10);
```
Be sure there are two periods in the range specification. Notice that the labels on the tick marks on both the *x*- and *y*-axes are integers.

*What happens when a common mistake is made in entering the **plot** command?*

```
plot(p, x = -2,3);
```
The error message indicates that there are invalid arguments. When you see such an error message, you should first check to be sure you have entered the domain and range using periods.

You can easily change the domain of your graph.

```
plot(p, x = -2..3, y = -10..10);
```
Changing the domain and range of your graphs allows you to explore the behavior of an expression.

Editing on Your Computer

You can use the powerful editing features of Maple to speed your work. (Verbal directions, in the text area on the right, appear in *italics*.)

*Copy the last **plot** statement.*

*Use the mouse to move the cursor to the beginning of the previous **plot** statement. Hold down the mouse button, drag the cursor to the end of the statement, and release the mouse button.*
You will have performed this action correctly if the entire **plot** statement is highlighted.

Now pull down the Edit menu by pointing at it and holding down the mouse button. Then select Copy by continuing to hold down the mouse button and dragging it down until Copy is highlighted. Release the mouse button.
An image of the **plot** statement is now saved.

You can paste this copied statement anywhere you wish in the Maple environment.

Move the cursor next to the last prompt and click the mouse button. Pull down the Edit menu and select Paste.
The **plot** statement should appear at the cursor position.

Edit this statement so that the domain of the plot is from −3 to 3.

To do this, move the cursor to the right of −2 in the **plot** *statement and click the mouse button. Now press the Backspace key to erase the 2. Type* **3** *and press Enter.*
Notice that you did not have to be at the end of the line for Maple to accept the entire statement when you pressed Enter.

If you pull down the Edit menu, you can see that special key combinations can be used to accomplish copying and pasting. For example, if you highlight a word, you can copy it by holding down the Ctrl key and pressing C on a Windows computer and the ⌘ key and C on a Macintosh. You can speed your work by using these key combinations. The Undo command in the Edit menu is very useful if you are surprised by an edit operation. You can use the keys with arrows on them on your keyboard or the mouse to move the cursor around the screen.

Ending a session.

Select the Quit item in the File menu.
You should normally end a session in this way.

Extensions

Help Facility   The Help facility in the Maple environment is extremely useful. You already know how to access it using the **?** symbol. Maple V allows you to access the Help facility by selecting Help in the main menu at the top of the screen. You should make a point of learning to get around in the Help facility and to consider using it anytime you have a question regarding commands, packages, and so on. For example, if you click on the Help menu, you will access a Help window. You can click on any underlined word in any Help window to access more information about that word. Experiment with this facility. Remember to close the Help windows by clicking on their Close boxes when you are finished with them.

The Main Menu and Tool Bar in the Maple V Environment
The Main menu items in the Maple V environment have a number of helpful features. Use the Save and Print items of the File menu to save and/or print your session. Use the icons in the Tool bar to access various features of the Maple environment. You can use Balloon Help in both the Windows and Macintosh environments to see what actions the icons represent. You activate the Balloon Help by clicking on the Question Mark (**?**) at the top right of the

screen and then selecting Show Balloons. A balloon describing the action of an icon appears when you move the cursor to that icon. You can turn off Balloon Help by selecting Hide Balloons in the Question Mark menu item.

Additional Activities

Entering Expressions Write each of the following expressions as you would enter them in Maple.

1. $\dfrac{1}{x-2}$

2. $\dfrac{1}{x} + \dfrac{5}{3x}$

3. $\dfrac{x-2}{x^4 - 3x^3 + 1}$

4. $\dfrac{x-4}{(x^2 - 2x - 7)^5}$

5. 2^x

6. 2^{x+5}

Exploring Expressions Explore the following expressions using the **solve**, **factor**, and **plot** commands.

7. $x^2 - 5x + 6$

8. $x^2 - 4x - 12$

9. $6x^2 + x - 15$

10. $40x^2 - 131x + 84$

11. $90x^2 - 249x + 168$

Exploring the Maple V Environment

12. Change the size of the commands you enter by using the x icons at the right of the Tool bar.

13. Cause the paragraph markers to appear by using the last icon on the Tool bar next to the x's.

14. Use the Exclamation Mark icon (**!**) to execute a command rather than pressing Enter or Return.

15. Insert a new prompt using the Insert Prompt (**[>**) icon.

16. Experiment with the **x** icon at the left of the Tool bar by entering a command and its semicolon but clicking on the **x** icon rather than pressing Enter or Return.

CHAPTER TWO
Precalculus Algebra

This chapter presents many of the commands available in the Maple environment that are useful in a typical precalculus course. The major topic in such a course is the study of functions: their definitions, domains and ranges, asymptotes, graphs, and behaviors. Maple is an extremely powerful tool in this study and in other precalculus topics as well.

2.1 Solving Equations

Polynomial Equations

You've seen how to solve some equations. Let's look at some more.

```
q := 3*x^2 - 5*x + 2;
solve(q = 0);
```

Here you are entering two statements. Press Enter after each statement. This is $3x^2 - 5x + 2 = 0$. Your screen should look something like this:

Use your factoring ability to check the solutions displayed.

Use **subs** *to check your result.*

```
subs(x = 1, q);
```
The displayed result of **0** indicates that the value of q when $x = 1$ is 0. In a similar manner, you can check that $x = \frac{2}{3}$ is a correct solution also.

Sometimes solutions are irrational numbers.

```
solve(x^2 - 3 = 0);
```
Maple uses the radical symbol for square roots only (except under DOS). Fractional exponents are used for most others.

You can solve equations whose solutions are more complicated expressions.

```
q := q - 1;
solve(q = 0);
```
The two displayed solutions are, as before, separated by a comma.

You may wish to have decimal approximations for these solutions.

```
fsolve(q = 0);
```
The number of digits in the decimal approximations will depend on the value of *Digits*.

You can solve the equation $3x^2 - 5x + 1 = 0$ in a way that takes longer but provides the details of the steps required. The Maple commands needed in the step-by-step method are located in the **student** package.

You access the student package using the **with** *statement.*

```
with(student);
```
The commands available in this package are displayed.

Now complete the square in x.

```
completesquare(q = 0, x);
```
In the equation returned, the left-hand side is displayed with the square completed.

You can isolate various parts of an equation.

```
isolate(", x - 5/6);
```
Notice that $x - \frac{5}{6}$ is isolated on the left side of the equation. However, the right side is not as nice as you would like it.

You can obtain the results in better form.

```
convert(", radical);
```
Your screen should look something like this:

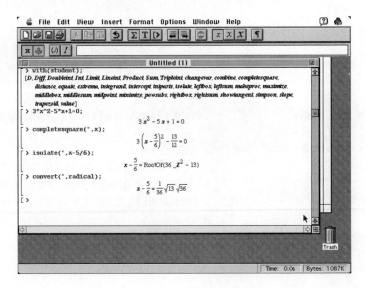

Now you can continue to think about the output.

Simplify the expression.

```
simplify(");
```
The results are now in a nicer form.

Now to the final solution.

```
isolate(", x);
```
The step-by-step process has many educational advantages but also requires some thought on your part to supply missing details, if any. In this case, the **isolate** command obviously does not give the plus and minus values when taking the square root.

Some equations have complex solutions.

```
solve(x^2 + 1 = 0);
```
The complex number i may be represented as I or **i**.

You can solve equations whose solutions are more involved complex expressions.

```
q := q + 6;
solve(q = 0);
```
You need to be careful to look for i's in solutions.

Again, you may wish to display the solutions in decimal form.

```
fsolve(q = 0);
```
The **fsolve** command finds only real number solutions.

The exact solutions can be approximated by decimals.

```
solve(q = 0);
```
This displays the same two exact complex solutions as before.

You can assign this sequence of solutions to a variable.

```
s := ";
```
Recall the **"** mark represents the most recent computed result.

The variable s is a sequence with two elements. You can access each solution separately.

```
evalf(s[1]);
```
Notice the brackets around 1. The **evalf** command returns the floating-point approximation of the first solution in the sequence.

You can access the second solution as well.

```
evalf(s[2]);
```
The variable *s* contains the sequence of solutions. The second element of this sequence is designated as **s[2]** in Maple. Brackets (rather than parentheses) are required.

You can solve polynomial equations of higher degree than 2. You begin by assigning the polynomial expression to a variable.

```
q := 6*x^4 - 35*x^3 + 22*x^2 + 17*x - 10;
```
This is $6x^4 - 35x^3 + 22x^2 + 17x - 10$.

You can now solve the equation q = 0.

```
solve(q = 0);
```
You know that a polynomial of degree 4 will have at most four solutions. This equation has four rational solutions.

A slightly different equation (q = 1) can give a much different result.

```
solve(q = 1);
```
Maple indicates the solution as **RootOf (6_Z^4 - 35_Z^3 + 22_Z^2 + 17_Z - 10)**. This is not a very useful form of the solution because it only tells you that the solutions of the equation are the roots of a particular polynomial—namely, 6Z^4 − 35Z^3 + 22Z^2 + 17Z − 10 (the original polynomial). You should not become overly concerned when such results occur because there are a number of ways to handle the situation, as you will see.

You can display the actual roots of polynomials of degree less than 5.

```
allvalues(");
```
The solutions are clearly very complicated. You can see that portions of the displayed solutions involve numbers with percent (%) signs attached, like %2. Maple uses such percented numbers to represent expressions when displaying complicated solutions like these. The values of the percented expressions appear after the solutions.

*You can use **plot** to graph the expression q − 1 to resolve these conflicting results.*

```
plot(q - 1, x = -1..2);
```
The places where this graph crosses the *x*-axis are the solutions of the equation $q - 1 = 0$. The graph shows three of the four real solutions that seem to correspond to the solutions obtained using **fsolve**. You can adjust the graph in the **plot** command to investigate this expression further. Here again, you use the power of Maple to check the results you obtained with Maple.

Other Types of Equations

You can solve many trigono-metric equations.

```
p := cos(x) - sin(x);
```
Notice that parentheses are required in using the trigonometric functions.

Now you can solve the equation p = 0, which is equivalent to $\cos(x) - \sin(x) = 0$.

```
solve(p = 0);
```
You may recall that trigonometric equations often have an infinite number of solutions. The solution displayed on the screen, $\frac{1}{4}\pi$ or $\frac{\pi}{4}$, may not be the only solution. The **solve** command usually returns a single solution to nonpolynomial equations even if there are many solutions.

Graphing the expression can help you determine the complete solution set.

```
plot(p, x = 0..2*Pi);
```
The symbol π is represented by Pi with a capital P. Notice that there is more than one solution.

*You can use the **fsolve** command to find other solutions.*

```
fsolve(p = 0, x, 1.5..4);
```
Notice the comma after **x**. The **1.5..4** indicates which interval **fsolve** searches for a solution. The number displayed should be a multiple of π.

What multiple of π is it?

```
evalf("/Pi);
```
Thus, the solution is approximately $\frac{5\pi}{4}$, which is π units from the previous solution. Can you write down the solution set in set notation based on this information?

You can solve logarithmic equations also.

```
solve(ln(x) + ln(x+1) = ln(2));
```
$\ln(x)$ is the natural logarithm of *x*. Thus, $\ln(2)$ is $\log_e(2)$ and is approximately 0.693172. The solution to the equation is given as 1. Logarithms to bases other than *e* can be entered using the standard conversion formula. For example,

$$\log_{10}(x) = \frac{\ln(x)}{\ln(10)}$$

Exponential equations are easy to enter and solve.

```
solve(2^x = 5);
```
The exact solution is displayed using natural logarithms. You use the **evalf** command to obtain a decimal approximation to the solution.

*Use **fsolve** to find an approximate solution to this equation.*

```
fsolve(2^x = 5);
```
Notice that the solution is different from the solution you obtained using **evalf**. Maple uses two different methods to obtain this approximate result. The results differ in the tenth place. Better approximations can be obtained by setting *Digits* to a larger integer value.

Inequalities

You can solve inequalities.

```
solve(x^2 - 5*x < 0);
```
The solution set for this inequality is the interval $(0, 5)$, or the set $\{x \mid 0 < x < 5\}$. The solution is displayed by Maple as **RealRange(Open(0), Open(5))**. You need to study the form of this output because it is Maple's way of indicating the intersection of two sets.

Maple uses a similar form to represent set union.

```
solve(x^2 - 5*x >= 0);
```
Notice how the $\geq$ symbol is entered in Maple. Maple displays **RealRange(-∞,0), RealRange(5,∞)**. The displayed solution uses **RealRange** twice to indicate the union of two sets. Be careful to look for these differences in notation when solving inequalities. Also, notice that Maple does not include the endpoints at 0 and 5 even though the inequality is $\leq$. As usual, you need to take into account such limitations.

You can also solve systems of equations.

```
solve({x+y=5,x-y=2}, {x,y});
```
Here, Maple solves a set of equations (in the first pair of braces),

$$x + y = 5$$
$$x - y = 2$$

for a set of variables (in the second set of braces). The solution set is displayed with an *x*-value and a *y*-value.

*Use **subs** to check your results.*

```
subs({y = 3/2, x = 7/2}, x+y=5);
```
Here, the values of *x* and *y* are substituted in the equation **x+y = 5**. The output **5 = 5** indicates that the point $(7/2, 3/2)$ satisfies the first equation. Check that this point satisfies the second equation as well.

You can check the solution of the system of equations graphically.

```
plot({5-x, x-2},x=-4..4);
```
Notice that you must write the equation $x + y = 5$ in the form $y = 5 - x$ and $x - y = 2$ in the form $y = x - 2$ to plot the graphs. Also, the braces are required when you plot a set of more than one function on the same axes.

A slight change in the equations gives a different result.

```
solve({x+y=5.,x-y=2}, {x,y});
```
Notice the decimal point after the 5 in the first pair of braces. Maple uses a numerical method that yields approximate solutions if one of the numbers in the system of equations is in floating-point format. In this case, the approximations have the same value as the exact rational solutions displayed in the previous item.

The Assume Command   The **assume** command allows you to specify conditions on variables. For example, if x is positive, then the equation $x^2 = 4$ has only one solution, $x = 2$.

Let's solve an equation involving square roots.

```
solve(sqrt(x^2)=2);
```
The solution to this equation is the two numbers -2 and 2. These are the values displayed.

Specify that x is positive.

```
assume(x>0);
```
The command instructs Maple that x is positive. We could have also chosen to tell Maple that x was a real number or that x was negative.

Let's solve the equation again.

```
solve(sqrt(x^2)=2);
```
This time the value 2 is displayed because it is the only positive value of x for which the equation is true.

You can reset x.

```
x:='x';
```
This command reestablishes x as a variable with no assigned value or restrictions. Resetting variables that have been restricted in some way with the **assume** command is a good practice, as you saw earlier.

Additional Activities

Explore the following polynomials using the **factor, solve, fsolve, evalf,** and **plot** commands.

1. $x^4 - x^3 - 5x^2 + 12$
2. $2x^3 - 13x^2 - 4x + 60$

3. $8x^2 + 2x^3 - x^4$

4. $2x^4 - 5x^3 + 10x - 12$

5. $x^5 - x^4 - 15x^3 + x^2 + 38x + 24$

6. $x^5 - x^4 - 15x^3 + x^2 + 38x + 10$

2.2 Rational Expressions

You can assign a rational expression to a variable.

```
r := 1/(x + 1) - 1/(x - 1);
```
Because you cannot enter horizontal fraction bars, you need to be careful to delineate the numerators and denominators clearly using parentheses. Fortunately, Maple displays this rational expression in standard two-dimensional format.

You can simplify this expression.

```
simplify(r);
```
Your screen should look something like this:

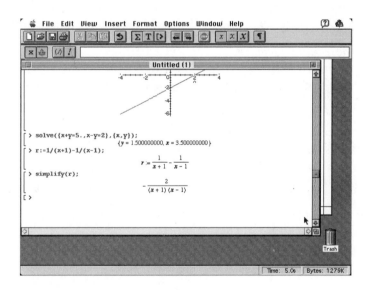

Maple adds the two rational expressions and displays the result in two-dimensional form.

*Extract the denominator from this expression using the **denom** command.*

```
denom(");
```
The denominator is displayed in factored form as it was displayed in the last item. You can use the **expand** command to display this denominator as a polynomial in standard form.

*The numerator can be extracted with the **numer** command.*

```
numer("");
```
Using **""** refers to the output before the last output (the second output back). The number -2 is the numerator of this rational expression.

*Graph this expression using the **plot** command.*

```
plot(r, x=-10..10);
```
From your experience in precalculus mathematics, you know that this expression should have asymptotes. However, the steep lines that appear to be asymptotes near -1 and 1 are only lines joining points on the graph.

For a graph of an expression, you can force Maple to plot just the points that it computes.

```
plot(r, x=-10..10, style = point
    symbol = POINT);
```
The possible symbols are **BOX**, **CIRCLE**, **CROSS**, **DIAMOND**, and **POINT**. The graph is now displayed without connecting the computed points. There are no apparent asymptotic lines on the displayed graph.

You can change the symbol used to plot the points.

```
plot(r, x=-10..10, style = point,
    symbol = CIRCLE);
```
This can sometimes help emphasize the graph.

*Use the **solve** command to determine where the asymptotes should be on the graph.*

```
solve(denom(r));
```
The two solutions give the location of the asymptotes. They can be checked against the graph of the expression.

Graph the expression with a smaller horizontal window that still includes the asymptotes.

```
plot(r,x=-2..2,y=-30..30,style = point,
    symbol = CIRCLE);
```
Maple now displays a graph that more closely represents the known features of the graph of the expression.

Let's look at another rational expression.

```
s:=(x^2 + 5*x + 6)/(x^3 + 2*x^2 - x - 2);
```
Notice the parentheses around the numerator and denominator of the expression

$$\frac{x^2 + 5x + 6}{x^3 + 2x^2 - x - 2}$$

You can factor both the numerator and denominator of this rational expression.

```
factor(numer(s));
factor(denom(s));
```
Here, you are entering two statements (pressing Enter after each statement). You can see that the numerator and denominator can be factored. Notice the factors of the denominator.

Simplify the expression **s**.

```
simplify(s);
```
Notice that the common factor has been divided out and the denominator expanded. You should be aware that this simplification is correct only if $x \neq -2$.

You can graph this expression.

```
plot(s, x=-3..3, y=-30..30, style=point,
    symbol = CIRCLE);
```
Notice that there is no vertical asymptote at $x = -2$, even though you saw that $x + 2$ was a factor of the denominator. There is no vertical asymptote at $x = -2$ because this factor divides out of both numerator and denominator. The Maple graph seems to be defined at $x = -2$, which is incorrect because the denominator is zero at $x = -2$. Maple simplifies an expression before graphing it. This can result in the loss of information. In this case, the graph will never show that the function is undefined at $x = -2$. You should continue to be aware of possible discrepancies between Maple graphs (which are just connected points) and actual graphs.

Additional Activities

Determine the zeros and asymptotes of the following rational expressions using the **factor** and **solve** commands.

1. $\dfrac{2x - 3}{x^2 - 9}$

2. $\dfrac{2x + 3}{x - 1}$

3. $\dfrac{x^2 - 2x - 8}{x^2 - 2x}$

4. $\dfrac{x^2 + 3x - 10}{4x + 20}$

5. $\dfrac{x^2 - 1}{x + 2}$

6. $\dfrac{x^2 - 1}{x^3 - 1}$

7. $\dfrac{2x^2 - 3x - 2}{x^2 - 5x}$

8. $\dfrac{x^2 - 2x + 1}{x^4 - 1}$

9. $\dfrac{4x^3 - 5x^2 + 3x - 6}{2x^2 + 3x + 5}$

10. $\dfrac{2x^3 - 7x^2 + 7x - 2}{2x^2 + 5x - 3}$

2.3 Defining Functions and Procedures

Functions of One Variable

You can use the Maple procedure facility to create function definitions. A procedure performs a task that is described in a set of instructions. A function is a procedure that returns a value specified by its set of instructions. You can use this facility to define functions such as:

$$f(x) = x^2 + 3x - 5$$
$$g(x) = \cos(x) - x\ln(x)$$
$$h(x) = \frac{\cos(x)}{x^2 + 3x - 21}$$

You can define the real-valued function f whose rule is $f(x) = x^2$.

```
f  :=   x -> x^2;
```
You enter the mapping arrow (->) by typing a minus sign (-) followed by a greater than symbol (>) with no space between them. The function is named f and maps or takes x to x^2. Thus, x^2 is the rule for the function. This procedure has one variable x and one task (to square x). It is a function because it returns exactly one value. Maple echoes the procedure definition when you enter this line.

You can obtain function values for f.

```
f(2);
```
This statement asks Maple to evaluate and display the function value of f at $x = 2$.

You can use variable names in a function evaluation.

`f(a+b);`
The value displayed is the value of f at $x = (a + b)$. You can use the **expand** command to display this function value without parentheses.

You can also use defined functions in algebraic expressions such as
$$\frac{f(x + h) - f(x)}{h}$$

`(f(x + h) - f(x))/h;`
Parentheses must be placed around the entire numerator because you are entering this expression on one line.

The value displayed can be simplified.

`simplify(");`
Maple removes the parentheses, combines like terms, and reduces fractions to lowest terms. Notice that the simplified expression is equivalent to the original expression as long as $h \neq 0$.

Consider the piecewise statement to define the function
$$f(x) = \begin{cases} x^2 & \text{if } x > 3 \\ x - 5 & \text{if } x \leq 3 \end{cases}$$

`piecewise(x > 3, x^2, x - 5);`
In this statement, if the domain value x is greater than 3, then $f(x)$ is determined by the rule x^2. However, if x is less than or equal to 3, then $f(x)$ is determined by the rule $x - 5$. Your screen should look something like this:

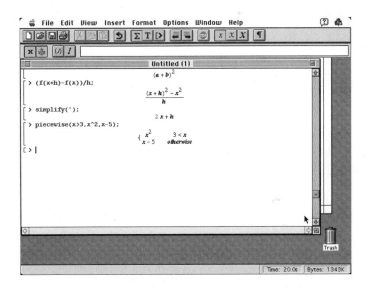

Notice that the expression could be the rule for a function, but it is not a function yet. You can define a piecewise function with this rule.

Define the piecewise func-tion.	```f := x -> piecewise(x > 3, x^2, x-5);```
	Notice that the fancy formatting does not appear in the output in this case.
You can obtain function values as before.	```f(2);``` ```f(5);```
	Remember to press Enter after each semicolon. You should check to make sure the function is using the appropriate rule in each case.
You can use **plot** *to graph this function.*	```plot(f);```
	Notice that the *x*-values of the window do not need to be specified when a function is defined as a piecewise function. Does the graph of the function clearly show the two pieces of the graph? You should graph this function, again using the style and symbol features (**CIRCLE**) in **plot** to see a more accurate representation of the function. You may have to select suitable domains to see the graph clearly in some complicated functions.
Unassign the definition of f.	```f := 'f';```
	This is similar to unassigning the value of a variable.

Functions of Several Variables

Functions of several variables occur in the latter part of the calculus sequence. They are written in mathematical notation much like one-variable functions. One example is

$$f(x, y) = x^2 + y^2 - 3$$

Define this function in Maple.	```f := (x,y) -> x^2 + y^2 - 3;```
	Here, each domain value of the function is an ordered pair of numbers (in parentheses) and the rule on the right of the mapping arrow uses two variables.
You can find values for such functions.	```f(2,5);```
	The function value for the pair of numbers $(2, 5)$ is $2^2 + 5^2 - 3$. The number displayed is 26.
Such functions can be plotted in three dimensions.	```plot3d(f, -2..2, -2..2);```
	Notice the characters **3d** appended to the **plot** command. This three-dimensional plot uses values for *x* and *y* in the *xy*-plane from -2 to 2 in both the *x*- and *y*-directions. Additional infor-

mation about three-dimensional graphing is covered at the end of Chapter 3.

Automating Commands in Maple

Frequently, you will want to repeat some particular command or set of commands several times with slightly different values. You do this with a looping structure using the **for** and **do** commands.

Print a table of values.

```
for k from 1 to 3 do print(k, k^2); od;
```
This prints out three pairs of numbers. Notice that the index moves from 1 to 3 by steps of 1. The command that is repeatedly performed is a **print** command and it is enclosed in the pair **do/od**.

Retype this line in more readable multiline form. You need to hold down the Shift key and press Enter at the end of the first three lines. Press Enter after the last line.

```
for k from 1 to 3
  do
    print(k, k^2);
  od;
```
The indentation in these lines is a structured format commonly used in programming. Pressing Shift and Enter moves the cursor to next line without executing the line. When you press Enter at the end of the last line, all the lines will be performed, causing three pairs of numbers to be displayed on the screen.

Modify this looping structure to step by one-half.

```
for k from 1 by .5 to 3
  do
    print(k, k^2);
  od;
```
Again, remember to hold down the Shift key and then press Enter at all but the last line; press only Enter after the last line to define this procedure. Notice that there are now five pairs of values because the step size is one-half. You may wish to use the editing capabilities of your computer rather than retyping the entire program.

An Automating Procedure

You can use this looping structure as part of a procedure. Such procedures are often called programs.

Define **maketable**.

```
maketable :=
  proc(n)
    for k from 1 by .5 to n
```

```
            do
               print(k, k^2);
            od;
         end;
```

Remember to press Shift–Enter at the end of every line but the last as you enter this procedure. The procedure **maketable** uses **n** as its argument. Press Enter to define this procedure. Notice that only a compact version of the procedure definition is displayed. Do not be concerned if a warning is displayed.

Let's use this procedure.

```
maketable(5);
```

As you might expect, a table of squares is displayed.

Generalizing the **maketable** *procedure.*

Change the second and third lines of the procedure definition as follows:

```
maketable :=
   proc(n, increment)
   for k from 1 by increment to n
     do
        print(k, k^2);
     od;
   end;
```

After you have made the changes, press Enter to define the procedure. Again, a compact version of the procedure is displayed.

Let's use this new procedure.

```
maketable(3, .2);
```

Are the values displayed those that you would expect? The step size is now .2 and the last pair is 3, 9.

Automated Plotting

You can define a procedure to plot several related functions on the same axis.

Graph a set of polynomials.

```
polyplot :=
   proc(n)
   polys := NULL;
   for k from 1 to n
     do
        polys := polys, x^k;
     od;
   plot({polys},x=-10..10,y =-10..10);
   end;
```

Press Enter to define the procedure. This procedure creates the polynomials in the **for/do** loop. The **plot** command displays this set of polynomials ({**polys**}) on the same axes.

Let's use this procedure.

```
polyplot(3);
```

Was the displayed plot what you expected? The straight line, quadratic, and cubic functions are graphed together.

You can generalize this procedure with additional arguments in many ways. For example, the domain and range values you wish to use in the graph can appear as arguments.

Extensions

Automating Commands The **for** and **do** commands allow you to repeat a process as many times as you need. For example, you could use the following commands to display the interest and amount paid toward the principal of a loan. The monthly payments on a loan of $8000 at 12% are $210.67 for 48 months.

```
prin := 8000;
months := 48;
for k from 1 to months
   do
     intr := prin * (12/1200);
     pay := 210.67 - intr;
     prin := prin - pay;
     print(intr, pay);
   od:
print('Principal remaining is', prin);
```

The colon after **od** is important if you wish to display only the interest and amount paid toward the principal. Otherwise, a semicolon will cause each of the assignment statements to be displayed everytime through the loop. It is also important to note that backquotes (`'`) are needed around a string that is to be displayed, as in the last **print** command. To execute this set of commands, you press Enter with the cursor somewhere in the program. Entering, defining, and executing programs can vary on different platforms. Check the Maple V manuals for your computer for details.

It is not difficult to generalize this routine into a program that will allow you to input the principal, rate, number of monthly payments, and the amount of each monthly payment. You can then display the monthly interest and amount paid toward the principal for the number of months chosen. Finally, you can display the principal remaining after making this number of monthly payments.

```
payment :=
  proc(p, rate, m, mopay)
  prin := p;
  months := m;
  for k from 1 to months
    do
       intr := prin * (rate/1200);
       pay := mopay - intr:
       prin := prin - pay;
       print(intr, pay);
    od:
  print('Principal remaining is',prin);
  end;
```

Once you enter this program, you can run it with various values as you wish. For example, to produce the same results as in the previous program, you would enter
```
payment(8000, 12, 48, 210.67);
```

Additional Activities

1. Enter the function $f(x) = \dfrac{x^2}{x^2 + 2}$ and graph it.

2. Enter the function of two variables $f(x, y) = x^2 + y^2$ and determine the value of the function at the points $(3, -2)$ and $(\sin(2), \cos(2))$.

3. Enter the function $f(x) = \text{sign}[\cos(x)]$. Graph this function. What values does this function take on most frequently?

4. Enter the function $f(x) = \dfrac{x^2 - 3x + 5}{\sin(x) + 1}$. Use Maple to determine whether this function is defined at $\dfrac{-11\pi}{2}$.

5. Develop and enter a function for the length of the line segment between two points (a, b) and (c, d). Use this function to determine the length of the line segment between $(2, 5)$ and $(-3, 7)$ and the length of the line segment between an arbitrary point (r, s) and $(2, 3)$. (Be sure to deassign all variables you use.)

2.4 Additional Plotting Features

The `plot` Command

The `plot` command has several options that allow you to create many types of graphs.

You may recall that Maple allows two or more functions to be graphed on the same axes.

```
plot({x^2,2*x + 5},x=-10..10);
```
You can change the interval of x-values if you wish to examine parts of these graphs (the intersections) more carefully by selecting suitable values of x.

Parametric Form

You can graph curves expressed in parametric form. For example, the two equations

$$x(t) = t - 1 \qquad \text{and} \qquad y(t) = t^2$$

give the x- and y-coordinates of a parabolic curve based on a parameter (dummy variable) t. If you solve these two functional equations for y in terms of x by eliminating the parameter t, you will find that $y = (x + 1)^2$, the equation of a parabola.

Use the `plot` command with special grouping symbols, `[ ]`, to graph the parametric curve just defined.

```
plot([t - 1, t^2, t=-2..2]);
```
Notice the placement of the brackets (`[ ]`) around the two parametric function rules and the specification of the domain of t.

Adjust the graph using the standard method for specifying the horizontal and vertical axes.

```
plot([t - 1,t^2,t=-2..2],-5..5,-2..10);
```
The curve still appears between -3 and 1 on the horizontal axis, because the parametric rule $t - 1$ (the first coordinate) has domain $[-2, 2]$. The axes, however, have values between $[-5, 5]$ horizontally and $[-2, 10]$ vertically. The function rules and the domain for the parameter t appear together inside the brackets, followed by the horizontal and vertical specifications for the graph. The x and y are not placed on the axes because they are omitted from the domain and range arguments.

You can graph more complicated curves using this parametric approach.

```
plot([t - sin(t),1 - cos(t),t=0..2*Pi]);
```
The parametric functions are $x(t) = t - \sin(t)$ and $y(t) = 1 - \cos(t)$. The domain of the parameter t is $[0, 2\pi]$. This curve is called a cycloid, which is easy to describe parametrically but is very complicated to describe in standard function form.

Polar Form

The parametric graphing feature allows you to graph functions in polar coordinates.

```
plot([sin(t),t, t=0..Pi],coords=polar);
```
This graphs the polar coordinate function $r = \sin(t)$. You may recall that this function describes a circle.

Some curves are more easily described using polar coordinates.

```
plot([1 + cos(t), t, t=0..2*Pi],
   coords=polar);
```
This graph is called a cardioid because it looks like a heart. It is the graph of $r = 1 + \cos(t)$.

Implicit Plotting

You can plot an equation in two variables without solving for one of them. For example, you can plot the unit circle, $x^2 + y^2 = 1$, by plotting the two functions $y = \pm\sqrt{1 - x^2}$. Maple, however, graphs the equation directly using the **implicitplot** command.

Let's plot the unit circle.

```
with(plots);
implicitplot(x^ 2 + y^ 2 = 1, x=-1..1,
   y=-1..1);
```
This command plots the expression $x^2 + y^2 = 1$ by creating a grid 25 by 25 in the graphics window from -1 to 1 horizontally and -1 to 1 vertically. It checks each point to see whether it almost satisfies the equation. Those points that almost satisfy the equation are plotted. You can use the options available with the **implicitplot** command to specify the number of points used in the grid. Use the Help feature for details on this and other options.

Animation

The family of functions $f(x) = ax^2$ is a set of parabolas. You can display the effect of the parameter a by displaying in sequence selected members in the family using the **animate** command.

Let's begin the animation process for this family of functions.

```
animate(a*x^2,x=-2..2,a=-5..5);
```
The displayed graph is the function $f(x) = -5x^2$, the first in a sequence of 16 function graphs based on a. The graphics window has $[-2, 2]$ as the interval of x-values. The a-values run from -5 to 5 at intervals of $\frac{10}{16}$ because there are 16 values of a in an interval of length 10.

Start the animation.

Click on the graph and then click on the second button of the new set of icons that appears.

When you click on the graph, a new row of icons appears near the top of the screen. These buttons control the animation of the graph. It would be helpful to click on each button to see what effect it has. The 16 graphs are displayed in order, giving an appearance of motion.

You can create more elaborate animations.

```
animate([k+5*cos(t),t,t=0..2*Pi],
    k=-9..-2,coords=polar);
```

The displayed graph is a polar coordinate graph of the cardioid $r = -9 + 5\cos(t)$. Once again, 16 graphs based on t can be displayed in sequence. Start the animation by clicking on the graph and then the second button.

2.5 Putting It All Together

In this section, you will use combinations of Maple commands you have learned to investigate polynomial and rational functions.

A Rational Function with Asymptotes

The graphs of rational functions can have interesting features such as horizontal, vertical, and oblique asymptotes. You can investigate these asymptotes by looking at the zeros of the denominators and at the behavior of the functions as the variable approaches $\pm\infty$. You will investigate the following rational function

$$f(x) = \frac{3x^3 - x^2 - 3x + 5}{x^2 - 2x - 1}$$

First you define the function.

```
f:=x -> (3*x^3-x^2-3*x+5)/(x^2-2*x-1);
```

Notice the parentheses around both the numerator and the denominator.

You can graph the function to obtain an overview of the behavior of the function.

```
plot(f);
```

Notice that with a function defined in this way, you do not need to specify the x-values for the graph. Looking at the graph, there appear to be one zero and two vertical asymptotes.

Restrict the domain to obtain more detailed information about the graph.

```
plot(f, -2..5);
```

This graph still doesn't seem to reveal enough information.

You can change the range as well.

```
plot(f, -2..5, -50..50);
```
The behavior of the function between the asymptotes is now more apparent. The seemingly vertical lines are, as you recall, calculated points that are connected. They are not truly asymptotes. You may wish to check this by using the **style = POINT** feature.

Determine the exact location of the vertical asymptotes.

```
solve(denom(f(x)) = 0);
```
The vertical asymptotes can occur only at the zeros of the denominator. The values displayed are exact, but how would you graph them on the *x*-axis?

You can find floating-point approximations for these two values.

```
fsolve(denom(f(x)) = 0);
```
Although exact values are useful at times, approximate values are also useful.

You may have noticed that the graph of the function seems to be a straight line away from the asymptotes.

```
quo(numer(f(x)), denom(f(x)), x);
```
Check to be sure there are sufficient parentheses that match. The **quo** command returns the polynomial part of the quotient. As you can see, this partial quotient is a linear rule.

You can check that this is an oblique asymptote.

```
plot({3*x + 5,f(x)},x=-10..10,y=-50..50);
```
Remember, plots can take a while depending on your computer. Is the graph of the function close to the line away from the asymptotes? Notice that the function graph intersects the oblique asymptote. You may wish to examine the graph more closely to the left of −5 by further adjusting the *x*- and *y*-values. You might try $x = -20..0$, $y = -20..10$.

You can also locate the x- and y-intercepts.

```
solve(f(x) = 0);
```
Once again, it is hard to tell what these possible *x*-intercept values are, but, if you look carefully, two of them are complex.

You can find an approximation of the real root.

```
fsolve(f(x) = 0);
```
Notice that this point is to the left of both asymptotes.

The y-intercept is easy to determine.

```
f(0);
```
The value of the *y*-intercept occurs when $x = 0$. You can easily make this computation in your head in this case.

Locate the intersection of the graph of the function and the oblique asymptote.

```
fsolve(3*x + 5 = f(x));
```
We laughed, too. Do you believe this answer? Can you check this answer using pencil and paper?

Finding the Roots of Polynomials

You can use the graphing, factoring, and equation-solving capabilities of Maple to investigate the roots of polynomials.

| *Let's look at a fifth-degree polynomial.* | ```
p := x -> 12*x^5 + 32*x^4 - 57*x^3 -
   213*x^2 - 104*x + 60;
``` |

This is $12x^5 + 32x^4 - 57x^3 - 213x^2 - 104x + 60$. Again, notice the use of the asterisk to indicate multiplication between coefficients and variables.

You can display this polynomial function.	`p(x);`

Maple displays the function in standard mathematical notation.

Graph this polynomial.	`plot(p);`

This graph gives few details of the behavior of the polynomial between -5 and 5. The graph of this polynomial, however, does appear to cross the x-axis between -5 and 5.

Focus your attention on a smaller interval.	`plot(p, -5..5);`

A few more details are discernible from this new graph. It shows that the polynomial may be zero at several points between -5 and 5. What is the largest value of a tick mark on the y-axis? You should think about restricting the y-values so that more detail will appear.

You know how to specify the second coordinate values.	`plot(p, -5..5, -10..10);`

There appear to be two zeros to the right of the origin and at least one zero to the left. Further investigation will show that this plot does not give an accurate picture of the behavior of the function. Such plots can occur because Maple uses only 50 points to start its plot of an expression.

Try a different set of y-values to investigate further the behavior of the polynomial.	`plot(p, -5..5, -100..100);`

This graph gives more information and seems to show the complete behavior of the function between -5 and 5. How many zeros do there appear to be? What is the degree of the polynomial?

You can magnify the graph of the function to the left of the origin.	`plot(p, -2.5..0, -10..10);`

It is more apparent that the graph just touches the x-axis at $x = -2$. You might reflect on why this graph is tangent to the x-axis.

Look at the graph to the right of the origin.	`plot(p, 0..3);`

The location of the first of the two zeros to the right of the origin can more easily be approximated now.

Try to factor this polynomial.	`factor(p(x));`

Maple has factored this polynomial completely. How many linear factors are there? Can you determine the exact values of the rational zeros of the polynomial?
```

Use the **solve** *command to determine the zeros of the polynomial.*

```
solve(p(x) = 0);
```
Notice that the zeros appear in the same order as the factors. How many times does -2 appear? How many times does the factor $(x + 2)$ appear?

You have used the **plot** command to investigate the behavior of the polynomial in a situation where all the zeros were rational.

Let's look at another polynomial.

```
q := x -> x^5 + 4*x^2 - 3*x + 5;
```
Be sure to enter the polynomial function carefully.

Graph the polynomial.

```
plot(q);
```
The graph seems to look the same as the first graph of *p* just given.

Graph the polynomial from −5 to 5.

```
plot(q, -5..5);
```
This time the polynomial seems to cross the *x*-axis once between -5 and 5.

You can get a better picture of the graph.

```
plot(q, -5..5, -100..100);
```
Now it is clear that the polynomial crosses the *x*-axis only once.

You can obtain a more detailed graph.

```
plot(q, -5..5, -10..10);
```
Some of the graph is cut off above the line $y = 10$. You can, however, see the behavior of the polynomial more clearly near its zero.

Let's factor the polynomial.

```
factor(q(x));
```
Surprise. Maple is unable to factor this particular polynomial. You know it must have at least one real zero from the Fundamental Theorem of Algebra. Thus, there should be at least one linear factor.

Hope is not lost. You can try the **solve** *command.*

```
solve(q(x)= 0);
```
The **RootOf** the same polynomial in *z* indicates that Maple could not find an exact solution.

Let's stay with it. You can try the **fsolve** *command.*

```
fsolve(q(x) = 0);
```
The approximate value is displayed. It is a negative value that matches the information on the graphs. Without further investigation, you might conclude that the other zeros are complex zeros. You might wish to examine the symbolic form of the polynomial to verify for yourself that there are no other real zeros outside the interval $[-5, 5]$.

The rational zeros of a polynomial can be found using the Maple **solve** or **factor** commands. Irrational and complex zeros are also sometimes found by Maple. Polynomials of high degree (5, 8, 10) can be difficult to investigate. The graphing approach is a very useful tool in such situations.

Let's look at one last example.

Enter the polynomial.

```
r:=x -> 2*x^5+11*x^4+2*x^3-51*x^2-14*x+60;
```
This is $2x^5 + 11x^4 + 2x^3 - 51x^2 - 14x + 60$. Be careful as you enter this polynomial.

You can factor first.

```
factor(r(x));
```
Maple factors this polynomial into linear and quadratic factors with integer coefficients. Can you determine the nature of the zeros?

*Use the **solve** command.*

```
solve(r(x) = 0);
```
All the zeros are displayed. How do they match up with the factors displayed before?

It might be interesting to graph this polynomial.

```
plot(r, -5..5, -100..100);
```
Does this initial graph give you information that matches the displayed zeros? You may wish to plot this polynomial for various values of x and y.

The **factor** and **solve** commands may give you all the information you need. When they don't, then it is useful to investigate the polynomial using the **plot** command. You need to be flexible in your use of these tools.

Additional Activities

Graph the following functions.

1. $x = \sin(t)$, $y = 2\cos(2t)$

2. $x = t^2$, $y = \cos(t)$

3. $x = t$, $y = t^2$

4. $r = 2\sin(3t)$

5. $r = 1 - 2\sin(t)$

6. $y = \cos(x)$

Graph the following functions, indicating their zeros and their horizontal and vertical asymptotes, if any.

7. $f(x) = \dfrac{2x^4 - 2x^2 + x + 5}{x^2 - 3x - 5}$

8. $f(x) = \dfrac{2x^4 + 7x^3 + 7x^2 + 2x}{x^3 - x + 51}$

9. $g(x) = \dfrac{2x^3 + 3x^3 + x^2 + 2}{x^3 - x^2 + 21}$

10. $p(x) = x(x^2 - 3)(x^2 - 8)$

11. $r(x) = 999x^3 + 780x^2 - 5428x + 3696$

12. $g(x) = \dfrac{x^5 - x^4}{x^5 - 6x^4 + 5x^3 + 26x^2 - 48x + 18}$

2.6   Matrices and Matrix Commands

The Maple operators you will need for this section are contained in the linear algebra package called **linalg**. You will need to load this package in order to study matrices and linear transformations and the solution of systems of linear equations.

*You use the **with** statement to access the **linalg** package.*

```
with(linalg);
```
The commands that are loaded into the Maple environment are displayed on the screen.

*You enter a matrix with the **matrix** command.*

```
A:=matrix(4,4,[[1,2,3,4],[2,3,0,-5],
[2,-1,1,1],[-2,2,0,-5]]);
```
The first two arguments of this command are the row and column dimensions of the array. The third argument of this command is the set of matrix entries. The bracketed sets of numbers represent the row entries of the matrix. Thus, the first row has four entries: $1, 2, 3, 4$. The fourth of the four rows has entries $-2, 2, 0, -5$. The bracketed row entries are nested inside brackets. Your screen should look something like this:

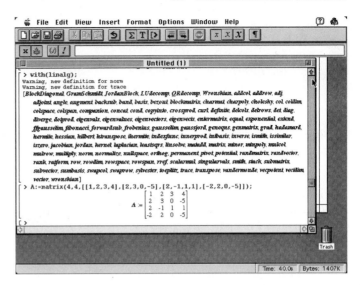

You can attempt to display the matrix.	`A;` Notice that **A** is returned. The array data structure is not displayed—only its name.
You can, however, display the matrix entries.	`evalm(A);` Notice that this command displays the matrix in standard row and column format.
Add two matrices.	`evalm(A + A);` Here you are adding the matrix *A* to itself. Notice that each entry of the displayed matrix is twice the corresponding entry of the matrix *A*.
You can interchange two rows.	`B := swaprow(A, 3, 4);` You may wish to display the matrix *A* again to compare it with *B*. Notice that this new matrix is assigned to *B*. The **swapcol** command is used to interchange two columns.
You can add A and B.	`evalm(A + B);` The last two rows of this matrix are the same.
Save this matrix for later use.	`C := ";` *C* is a 4 × 4 matrix whose last two rows are the same.
You can add a multiple of one row to another.	`addrow(C, 1, 2, m);` Notice that row 2 is replaced by *m* times the elements of row 1 plus the elements in row 2.

Find the inverse of A.	`inverse(A);` The exact values of the inverse are displayed.
You can check the inverse computation.	`evalm(A &* ");` As you would expect, a 4×4 identity matrix with 1s on the main diagonal is displayed.
Maple can transpose matrices.	`transpose(A);` You may wish to display A to check the result. Notice that the rows of A have become the columns of the transposed matrix.
The determinant of a matrix is easily obtained.	`det(A);` The determinant is a multiple of the denominators of the inverse matrix.

You may recall that the determinant of a matrix with two identical rows is zero.	`evalm(C);`
	`det(C);`
	As you might suspect, the determinant is 0. What should this imply for the inverse of C?

You can attempt to compute the inverse of C.	`inverse(C);` An error message is displayed because the matrix is singular.

Additional Activities

1. Find the inverse, transpose, and determinant of the following matrix:

$$\begin{bmatrix} 3 & 2 & 4 \\ 4 & -2 & 6 \\ 8 & 3 & 5 \end{bmatrix}$$

2. Find the inverse, transpose, and determinant of the following matrix:

$$\begin{bmatrix} 7 & -8 & 1 & 2 \\ 21 & 4 & 3 & -1 \\ -35 & 8 & 3 & -2 \\ 14 & 16 & 0 & 1 \end{bmatrix}$$

3. Solve the following system of equations:

$$3w + x + 7y + 9z = 4$$
$$w + x + 4y + 4z = 7$$
$$w + 2y + 3z = 0$$
$$2w + x + 4y + 6z = -6$$

4. Let

$$A = \begin{bmatrix} 1 & 3 & -2 \\ -4 & 1 & 5 \\ 2 & 3 & -1 \end{bmatrix}$$

Find the determinant and the determinant of the transpose of A.

5. Find the determinant of the matrix

$$A = \begin{bmatrix} 1 & 2 & 3 \\ 4 & 5 & 6 \\ 7 & 8 & 9 \end{bmatrix}$$

Use the **addrow** command to change A by first replacing row 2 with -4 times the first row added to the second row and then replacing row 3 with -7 times row 1 added to the third row. Finally, replace row 3 with -2 times row 3. Is the bottom row of the modified matrix all zeros? Does this fact verify the determinant value you obtained with the **det** command?

6. Find the transpose of both A and A^{-1}, where

$$A = \begin{bmatrix} 3 & 2 & -5 \\ -1 & 4 & 2 \\ 2 & -3 & 1 \end{bmatrix}$$

How do they compare?

CHAPTER THREE
Calculus

3.1 Calculus I

Maple contains a number of calculus commands or operators. These include differentiation, integration, and limit-taking commands.

Limits of Functions

You can take the limit of a function as the variable approaches a fixed number for a defined function f.

```
f := x -> (x^2 - 4) / (x - 2);
limit(f(x), x = 2);
```
Your screen should look like this:

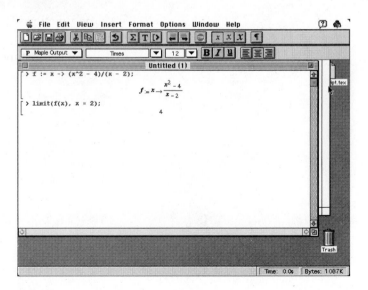

This is $\lim\limits_{x \to 2} f(x)$, where $f(x)$ is defined to be

$$\frac{x^2 - 4}{x - 2}$$

Notice that $x = 2$ indicates the value that the variable x will approach. The displayed value is the limit. You can see that this function is undefined at $x = 2$, but the limit exists there.

Graph the function to check if this limit seems correct.

```
plot(f, -5..5);
```
Notice that the graph appears to be a straight line even though you know that the function is undefined at $x = 2$. Can you draw an accurate graph of this function on the interval $[1, 3]$? Does the limit displayed before appear to be correct?

Factor the function as an additional check.

```
factor(f(x));
```
Can you explain why this factored form is not an accurate replacement of $f(x)$? Look at the definition of f and observe that it is undefined at $x = 2$. Is the factored representation undefined at $x = 2$?

You can find limits of more complicated functions.

```
f := x -> (x - 4)/(sqrt(x) - 2);
limit(f(x), x = 4);
```
The function

$$f(x) = \frac{x - 4}{\sqrt{x} - 2}$$

is not defined at $x = 4$. Does the limit displayed seem correct?

Graph the function to check the answer.

```
plot(f, 0..5);
```
Once again, the function graph is slightly flawed. Can you draw the correct graph of the function? Does the graph resemble a straight line or is it curved (except at $x = 4$)?

You must remember that the **plot** command in Maple computes only a finite number of points and then draws a smooth curve joining the points. Thus, it can incorrectly represent the graph of a function at or near points of discontinuity where the function is undefined.

You can determine limits at infinity as well.

```
g := x -> sqrt(x^2 - 4*x) - x;
limit(g(x), x = infinity);
```
Here you are looking at $\lim\limits_{x \to \infty} g(x)$. Try rationalizing the numerator using

$$\sqrt{x^2 - 4x} + x$$

to check the result displayed by Maple.

*Use the **plot** command to examine the behavior of the function for large values of x.*

```
plot(g, 0..100);
```
The number 100 is not a very large value for *x*, but the graph gives you a feel for the behavior of the function.

You can use much larger values of x to obtain more information about the function.

```
plot(g, 100..1000);
```
The function seems to be flattening out. What value is the function approaching for values of *x* near 1000? Does this agree with the value given by Maple and the value you calculated?

Limits of Piecewise-Defined Functions   You can examine piecewise-defined functions at the points where their rules change. At these points, you use Maple's ability to determine left and right limits.

Start by defining and simplifying the function

$$f(x) = \begin{cases} x - 1 & \text{for } x < 0 \\ x^2 & \text{for } x \geq 0 \end{cases}$$

```
f := x -> piecewise(x <= 0, x - 1, x^2);
simplify(f(x));
```
First, the definition is echoed, and then the piecewise function is given symbolically in standard notation, indicating where the discontinuity might occur.

Graph f.

```
plot(f, -2..2);
```
The **plot** function uses just the function name, *f*. The discontinuity is clearly shown at *x* = 0 by the graph. Can you sketch the graph of *f* using open and closed dots to indicate accurately the behavior of the function at *x* = 0?

You can use one-sided limits to determine

$$\lim_{x \to 0^-} f(x) \text{ and } \lim_{x \to 0^+} f(x)$$

```
limit(f(x), x = 0, left);
limit(f(x), x = 0, right);
limit(f(x), x = 0);
```
Does this function have a limit at *x* = 0?

Derivatives of Functions

Maple can differentiate most elementary functions.

*The differentiation command is **diff**.*

```
diff(3*x^4 - 4*x^2 - 5, x);
```
You should have no problem checking the displayed result. Notice that it is necessary to indicate that you are differentiating the expression that defines a function with respect to *x*.

You can differentiate piecewise functions.

```
diff(f(x), x);
```
The piecewise function *f(x)* was defined above. Can you verify that the displayed function is the derivative of *f(x)*?

You can differentiate the quotient of functions.

```
diff((x + 1)^2 / (x^2 + 2*x)^2, x);
```
The function being differentiated is

$$\frac{(x + 1)^2}{(x^2 + 2x)^2}$$

The result can be simplified.

Investigating a Function Using `plot` and `diff`

You can investigate the behavior of a function by graphing it. The information you garner from graphs of the function in conjunction with the zeros of its first and second derivatives can give you accurate approximations of the maxima, minima, and points of inflection. Consider the function

$$f(x) = \frac{x + 2}{3 + (x^2 + 1)^3}$$

You begin by entering the function as an expression.

```
f := (x + 2)/(3 + (x^2 + 1)^3);
```
The parentheses are needed in the numerator and denominator to ensure that Maple performs the operations in the order intended. This is a difficult function to investigate using pencil-and-paper methods.

Graph the function.

```
plot(f, x= -5..5);
```
Notice that the function seems to appear in the vicinity of -2 and seems to disappear in the vicinity of 2 and that the maximum value is less than 1.

Regraph the function with your own values for x and y.

```
plot(f, x=-5..5, y=-0.01..0.01);
```
The y-values are indicated as -0.01 and 0.01 to avoid the possible confusion that might occur with multiple dots between the numbers. You can see now that the graph crosses the x-axis near -2. Does there appear to be a point of inflection to the left of this minimum? If your graph is in a separate Plot window, you should click on the Maple Sessions window rather than closing the Plot window.

You can determine where maxima, minima, and points of inflection occur by looking at the derivatives of $f(x)$.

```
d := diff(f, x);
simplify(d);
fsolve(numer("));
```
These three statements give the first derivative and the approximate zeros for the numerator of $f'(x)$. These are, of course, the zeros of $f'(x)$. Refer back to the last graph by clicking on the last Plot

window; you can see that the negative number is the position of the minimum for the function. DOS users need to use the uparrow key to recall the last plot statement and redraw the graph.

Now for the points of inflection.

```
diff(d, x);
simplify(");
fsolve(numer("));
```

The expression *d* is the rule for $f'(x)$. Thus, **diff(d, x)** is the expression representing the second derivative of $f(x)$. Once again, you solve the numerator of the second derivative to reduce the amount of work that Maple has to do. This can cause problems if the denominator has real zeros.

Vertical tangent lines and cusps have not been considered here because the graphs did not seem to indicate them. How would you check to make sure there are no vertical tangent lines? Also, you might wish to know about horizontal and vertical asymptotes. You can investigate these using the **limit** command.

You have been working with a very difficult function whose most interesting behavior occurs very close to the *x*-axis. This would be very difficult to discover using pencil-and-paper methods. However, the combination of refining graphs and considering derivatives provides tools to allow you to understand thoroughly the behavior of the function. The analytical skills you can develop investigating such difficult functions with Maple will pay big dividends for you in any quantitative work you do in the future.

Implicit Differentiation

Sometimes, when the relationship between two variables is represented in an equation, you cannot explicitly represent one variable as a function of the other. You can compute the rate of change of one variable with respect to the other implicitly using the Maple **implicitdiff** command.

You can find the rate of change of y with respect to x for the unit circle.

```
implicitdiff(x^2 + y^2 = 1, y, x);
```

The equation of the unit circle is $x^2 + y^2 = 1$ and is the first argument of the **implicitdiff** command. The second argument, *y*, is the dependent variable, and the third argument, *x*, is the independent variable. Thus, you are considering *y* to be a function of *x* and $\frac{dy}{dx}$ is the rate of change of *y* with respect to *x* and is $\frac{-x}{y}$. Implicit differentiation is clearly useful in more complicated equations.

Integrals of Functions

Maple can determine indefinite and definite integrals of functions. Maple also has the ability to approximate definite integrals for functions whose antiderivative cannot be determined.

Integrals of polynomials are straightforward.

`int(3*x^4 - 2*x, x);`
You must indicate the variable of integration as with differentiation. Can you check the result displayed? *Hint:* Do you remember the **diff** command? Notice that a specific antiderivative is given, not the most general antiderivative. The constant of integration is not displayed.

Maple can integrate trigonometric functions such as $f(x) = \sec^4(x)$.

`int(sec(x)^4, x);`
Notice the placement of the exponent. Can you check the result?

Maple can perform integration by parts.

`int(x^3 * ln(x), x);`
You can use **diff(", x);** to check the result.

You can compute more complicated integrals such as

$$\int \frac{x^2}{\sqrt{x^2 - 9}} \, dx$$

`int(x^2 / sqrt(x^2 - 9), x);`
Be careful when you enter this expression.

You can check this result.

`diff(", x);`
This does not look anything like the original integrand.

You can, however, simplify this expression.

`simplify(");`
Check carefully to make sure this matches the original integrand.

Finally, you can integrate functions such as

$$\frac{x^2 + 2x + 1}{(x^2 + 1)^2(x - 2)}$$

`int((x^2+2*x+1)/((x^2+1)^2*(x - 2)), x);`
Clearly, you need to be careful when entering long expressions on one line. Remember, when you check this result, that you may need to use the **simplify** command.

Definite Integrals of Functions of One Variable

You can also evaluate definite integrals such as

$$\int_0^{\pi/2} \sin(x) \, dx$$

`int(sin(x), x = 0..Pi/2);`
Once again, notice the double dots between **0** and **Pi/2**. The result of this computation is 1, so the graph of one hump of the sine function is 2. Maple V is able to evaluate many definite integrals exactly, as in this case. However, you should be aware that not all definite integrals can be computed exactly by paper-and-pencil techniques or by using computer software.

The student Package

The **student** package for calculus, available with Maple, allows you to determine the solutions to certain problems in a step-by-step fashion rather than by simply applying a single Maple command. This is very useful when you wish to learn the solution process or to see more deeply into the structure of a problem.

To use the student package for calculus, you must first load it.

```
with(student);
```
This makes the commands in this package available.

Let's look at an indefinite integral that can be evaluated using the integration by parts method.

```
Int(x*sin(x), x);
```
This is the integral $\int x \sin(x)\, dx$. The **Int** operator with a capital **I** creates the integral but does not evaluate it.

Apply the integration by parts command.

```
intparts(", x);
```
The previous output (**"**) is integrated by parts. The **x** in the Maple statement is your choice of which factor in the integrand is to be differentiated. You can see that the result contains an integral that is standard and easily integrated.

You can investigate more complicated integrals.

```
intparts(Int(x^2*exp(2*x),x),x^2);
```
This is the integral $\int x^2 e^{2x}\, dx$. The result includes an integral that appears simpler than the original. This should encourage you to apply the integration by parts method again.

Apply the method again and choose the expression that is to be differentiated.

```
intparts(Int(x*exp(2*x),x),x);
```
You should be able to recognize the integral in this result. The factor 2 needs to be inserted in the integrand (with appropriate adjustment) to make it a standard form. You can now finish the problem. You will notice that the signs and multipliers that result from the integration by parts method need to be accounted for. You may find it easier to do this yourself by hand.

The **student** package also allows you to go through the step-by-step procedure used in the trigonometric substitution method.

You start with an integral.

```
Int(x^3*sqrt(1 - x^2), x);
```
Notice again that the integral is displayed and has not been evaluated. That is the difference between the **Int** and **int** commands. As you saw before, **int** evaluates integrals, whereas **Int** gives the unevaluated form of the integral.

You decide to use trig substitution.

```
changevar(x = sin(v), ", v);
```

The substitution of sin(*v*) for *x* is made in $\int x^3 \sqrt{1-x^2}\,dx$ and displayed.

Trig identities are necessary with this method.

```
powsubs(1 - sin(v)^2 = cos(v)^2, ");
```

The **powsubs** command allows you to replace $1 - \sin^2(v)$ with $\cos^2(v)$ in the last expression (**"**).

Because the radical is $\sqrt{\cos^2(v)}$, you can substitute cos(v) for it (assuming cos(v) is positive).

```
powsubs(sqrt(cos(v)^2)=cos(v),");
```

The result now involves only positive integer powers of sin(*x*) and cos(*x*).

Because the sine function is raised to an odd power, you can write it as the product of sin(v) times an even power of sin(v) and change the even powers of sine to cosine.

```
powsubs(sin(v)^2 = 1 - cos(v)^2, ");
```

You may already see the power forms in the displayed results. If not, use the **simplify** command.

*The **value** command in the student package finds the value of the unevaluated expression.*

```
value(");
```

The evaluated integral is displayed but is not in terms of *x*. You can use the **subs** command to accomplish this, but it is probably just as easy for you to perform the substitution by hand.

Investigating a Practical Problem

You can use Maple to help you solve real-world problems that require extensive and complicated symbolic computations. For example, suppose you wish to determine the longest ladder that can fit around a right angle turn in a hallway if it is held horizontally. The following diagram summarizes the information you are given to solve this problem:

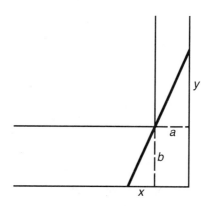

The widths of the two corridors of the hallway are labeled a and b. Using the two small right triangles, you find that the length of the ladder is $\sqrt{(x+a)^2 + (y+b)^2}$ and, from similarity, the equation $\frac{y}{a} = \frac{b}{x}$ is satisfied by the labeled lengths.

Assign the length of the ladder to the variable **ladder**.

```
ladder := sqrt((x+a)^2+(y+b)^2);
```
In this expression, x and y are variables and a and b are constants, or parameters, that describe a particular hallway. The expression defines a function of two variables.

Enter the similarity-based equation.

```
y/a = b/x;
```
This equation will be used to find y as a function of x.

Solve for y in terms of x.

```
solve(", y);
```
With this information, you can transform the expression for the length of the ladder from an expression in the two variables x and y into an expression in the single variable x.

Substitute the value of y in the **ladder** *expression.*

```
ladder := subs(y = ", ladder);
```
This result is an expression in one variable and defines a function of x with a and b as two constants, or parameters.

Determine the extrema of this function by finding its critical points.

```
diff(ladder, x);
simplify(");
solve(numer(") = 0, x);
```
There are four critical points, two are real and two are complex. Because a is a length, the critical point $-a$ does not provide a solution. The other real critical value is a surprisingly simple expression in the parameters a and b. But is this value for x a maximum or a minimum?

Investigate the second derivative.

```
diff(ladder, x$2);
simplify(");
```
The $x\$2$ calls for the second derivative. You can see that the second derivative is always positive by inspection. Thus, the ladder function is always concave up and the critical point gives rise to an absolute minimum for the function. How can this be?

Look carefully at the diagram and consider how ladders of various lengths would appear in it. Each ladder touches at the corner of the turn and at the walls in both corridors. The maximum length of a ladder that can negotiate the turn is the minimum length of ladders that can touch the corner and at the same time touch a wall in each corridor. You can determine particular ladder length values for given values of a and b by using the **subs** command with the expression for the critical point.

It should be noted that a different labeling of the diagram will lead to equations that are not so easily solved by Maple. For example, the labeling in the following diagram will lead to an expression in x or y, the zeros of whose derivative cannot be found exactly by Maple.

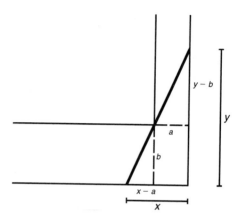

Also, because parameters a and b are used, numerical approximation techniques will not work either. Thus, you can use Maple to help you solve problems, but at each step you must think and consider ways to make a difficult computation less arduous both for yourself (with paper-and-pencil methods) and the computer software you are using.

You may wish to redo the Maple computations with fixed values for the corridor widths. For example, you might set $a = 3$ ft and $b = 4$ ft to get a feel for how the computations work. You may also wish to check the reasonableness of your analysis with corridors of equal length where $a = b$.

3.2 Calculus II

Series

You can find the value of sums such as $\sum_{i=1}^{5} i^2$, create a Taylor series for a differentiable function, and create power series using recursive formulas.

You can sum a finite series.

```
sum(k^2, k = 1..5);
```
Here the function is the first argument and the range of the index values is second.

The last value for the index can be a variable.

```
sum(k^2, k = 1..n);
```
Notice that this formula is equivalent to the standard one you encountered in precalculus mathematics or in the introduction to integration in your calculus course.

You can find some infinite sums as well.

```
sum(1/2^k, k = 1..infinity);
```
Because this is a geometric series, Maple can determine the sum.

Taylor Series

A function that is infinitely differentiable can be represented by a infinite series called a Taylor series. The **taylor** command displays a specified number of terms of the Taylor series expanded about a specified value.

The function e^x is infinitely differentiable.

```
taylor(exp(x), x = 0, 5);
```
Note the comma after 0. The Taylor series is expanded about $x = 0$, and the first five terms are displayed. Notice the last term displayed. $O(5)$ gives an indication of the degree to which the finite polynomial is inexact.

The Taylor series for more complicated functions can easily be obtained.

```
s := taylor(exp(-x)*cos(x), x = 2, 7);
```
Here the Taylor series is expanded about $x = 2$ and seven terms are requested. Notice that the last term displayed is $O(7)$, indicating the degree of accuracy of the approximation. You may wish to graph the function and its approximation as a visual check of how well the function is approximated.

Graph the function and its Taylor series approximation.

```
sp := convert(s, polynom);
plot({exp(-x)*cos(x),sp},x=-2..5);
```
Here, **convert** converts the Taylor series approximation into a polynomial by eliminating the order term. Notice that the graphs diverge to the left of 0 and to the right of 4.

Functions of Several Variables

Maple can determine the limit of a function of several variables. Maple can also find partial derivatives and multiple integrals of functions of several variables.

Derivatives of Functions of Several Variables

You can find the partial derivatives of $f(x, y) = x^2y^3 + e^x + \ln(y)$.

```
diff(x^2*y^3 + exp(x) + ln(y), x);
```
This yields the partial derivative of the function with respect to x:

$$\frac{\partial f(x, y)}{\partial x}$$

The partial derivative of
$f(x, y) = x^2y^3 + e^x + \ln(y)$
*with respect to y can also
be computed.*

```
diff(x^2*y^3 + exp(x) + ln(y), y);
```
This yields the partial derivative of the function with respect to y:

$$\frac{\partial f(x, y)}{\partial y}$$

*As you might expect, you
can find second partial
derivatives.*

```
diff(diff(x^2*y^3 + cos(x)*sin(y),x),y);
```
This is

$$\frac{\partial^2 f(x, y)}{\partial x \partial y}$$

A shorthand version of this command is:

```
diff(x^2*y^3 + cos(x)*sin(y), x, y)
```

You can determine other partial derivatives in the same way.

Applications of Partial Derivatives

Partial derivatives are used to compute the divergence and curl,
two frequently used tools in science and engineering. A vector
function **F** of three variables can be described by $\mathbf{F}(x, y, z) =$
$M(x, y, z)\mathbf{i} + N(x, y, z)\mathbf{j} + P(x, y, z)\mathbf{k}$, where $\mathbf{i}, \mathbf{j}$, and $\mathbf{k}$ are the unit
vectors in the positive x, y, and z directions, respectively. If M, N,
and P are differentiable functions, then the divergence of **F** is the
scalar function

$$\text{div } \mathbf{F} = \frac{\partial M}{\partial x} + \frac{\partial N}{\partial y} + \frac{\partial P}{\partial z}$$

and the curl of **F** is the vector function

$$\text{curl } \mathbf{F} = \left(\frac{\partial P}{\partial y} - \frac{\partial N}{\partial z} \right)\mathbf{i} + \left(\frac{\partial M}{\partial z} - \frac{\partial P}{\partial x} \right)\mathbf{j} + \left(\frac{\partial N}{\partial x} - \frac{\partial M}{\partial y} \right)\mathbf{k}$$

   Maple allows you to obtain these results easily. Consider
finding the divergence and curl of the vector function $\mathbf{F}(x, y, z) =$
$xy \sin(z)\mathbf{i} + x^2 \cos(y)\mathbf{j} + z\sqrt{xy}\,\mathbf{k}$. In order to invoke the divergence and curl commands, you need to load the linear algebra
package, **linalg**. Linear algebra is covered in much greater detail later in the book.

*First load the linear algebra
package.*

```
with(linalg);
```
The commands available in this package are displayed.

*Enter the components of the
function as a list.*

```
F := [x*y*sin(z),x^2*cos(y),z*sqrt(x*y)];
```

Next, enter the vector with respect to which the divergence and curl will be taken.

```
v := [x, y, z];
```
This vector is also entered as a list.

Now for the divergence of **F**.

```
diverge(F, v);
```
The divergence of **F** is displayed.

Finally, you can compute the curl of **F**.

```
curl(F, v);
```
The curl of **F** is displayed. You can see how rapidly Maple returns these results. You can also see how partial derivatives are used in the definitions of two commonly used functions used in science and engineering.

3.3   3D Plotting and Functions of Several Variables

This section introduces three-dimensional graphing. You will learn how to represent graphs in a variety of ways.

Graphing Functions of Two Variables

Graphing the function $f(x, y) = x^2 + y^2$.

```
plot3d(x^2 + y^2, x = -3..3, y = -3..3);
```
Here, the x and y intervals refer to the rectangle of domain values for the function defined by the expression $x^2 + y^2$. The range values (for z) are not specified and they will be computed automatically by Maple. The figure graphed is part of an elliptic paraboloid.

Use the **view** *option to specify the range.*

```
plot3d(x^2 + y^2, x = -3..3, y = -3..3,
   view = 0..10);
```
The interval of range values for the vertical dimension is [0, 10]. The plot looks substantially different.

Let's explore the amazing features of the Maple3d plot window. Several menus at the top of the window can be used to change the way the plot is displayed. But first you will adjust the viewing angle using the figure rotation feature. DOS users need to use the selections at the bottom of the screen and the Menu made available by the F10 key to accomplish the following tasks.

Let's rotate the figure forward.

Place the arrow cursor on the figure. Click the mouse button and notice that a box appears. Move the cursor straight up about half an inch by pressing the mouse button, dragging the mouse, and releasing it. Press Enter to redraw the figure.
Notice that you are seeing mostly the outside of the figure with a glimpse of its interior.

Change the **Style** *of the graph.*	*Pull down the* **Style** *menu and select* **Wireframe**. *Press Enter to redraw the figure.*

Three-dimensional plots are often difficult to display in a meaningful way. You will frequently need to adjust the way a figure is displayed to get a good visualization of the behavior of the function. You are encouraged to use the numerous options available in three-dimensional graphing as you investigate two-variable functions.

Display the axes.	*Select* **Normal** *from the* **Axes** *menu and redraw the figure.* The three axes along with units are displayed.
Let's look at one more view.	*Select* **Constrained** *under the* **Projection** *menu and* **Boxed** *under the* **Axes** *menu. Redraw the figure.* The figure changes substantially and is now well inside its box boundaries. As you can see, these options can change the figure dramatically.
Let's plot another function.	`plot3d(x^2 - y^2, x = -3..3, y = -3..3);` Place the arrow cursor somewhere on the figure and click the mouse button. Select **Patch** under the **Style** menu and redraw. This figure is called a saddle for obvious reasons. You should rotate it to see which views give you the most information. You may wish to select **Wireframe** under the **Style** menu to speed up the plots. The constrained view of this figure may give you some additional insight about the function as well.
One last plot.	`plot3d(x*exp(-x^2 - y^2), x = -2..2,` `    y = -2..2);` This figure is very interesting to play with. Enjoy!

Multiple Integrals of Functions of Several Variables

You can integrate

$$\int_0^1 \int_0^{\sqrt{1-x}} xy^2 \, dy \, dx$$

`int(int(x*y^2,y=0..sqrt(1-x)),x = 0..1);`
The fraction displayed is the exact value of this double integral. Triple integrals follow this same form.

An Application Using Multiple Integrals

You can find the center of mass of a plane lamina using multiple integrals. For example, suppose you wish to find the center of mass of a plane lamina in the shape of the region described by

$$0 \le x \le 4, \quad 0 \le y \le \sqrt{x}$$

if the density is given by $\rho(x, y) = xy$. You need to recall that the center of mass, $(\bar{x}, \bar{y})$, is

$$\bar{x} = \frac{M_y}{M} \quad \text{and} \quad \bar{y} = \frac{M_x}{M}$$

where M is the total mass of the lamina and M_x and M_y are the moments of the region with respect to the x-axis and y-axis, respectively.

You start by finding the total mass, M.

```
M:=int(int(x*y, y=0..sqrt(x)),x=0..4);
```
This is the double integral $M = \int_0^4 \int_0^{\sqrt{x}} xy \, dy \, dx$.

Next, find the moment of the region about the x-axis, M_x.

```
Mx:=int(int(x*y^2,y=0..sqrt(x)),x=0..4);
```
This is the double integral $M_x = \int_0^4 \int_0^{\sqrt{x}} y(xy) \, dy \, dx$.

Now for the moment of the region about the y-axis, M_y.

```
My:=int(int(x^2*y,y=0..sqrt(x)),x=0..4);
```
This is the double integral $M_y = \int_0^4 \int_0^{\sqrt{x}} x(xy) \, dy \, dx$.

You can now calculate the center of mass, $(\bar{x}, \bar{y})$.

```
xbar := My/M;
ybar := Mx/M;
```
The center of mass is found to be $(\bar{x}, \bar{y}) = (3, \frac{8}{7})$.

Moments of inertia of a plane lamina and the radius of gyration about an axis can be found in a similar fashion. You need but recall the formulas and perform the appropriate integrations.

Limits of a Function of Several Variables

You can take the limit of a function of two (or more) variables as (x, y) approaches (a, b).

```
limit((x^2 - y^2)/(x^2 + y^2), {x=0,y=0});
```
This is

$$\lim_{(x,y)\to(0,0)} \frac{x^2 - y^2}{x^2 + y^2}$$

Maple returns "undefined." The limit does not exist because the limit along the y-axis is different from the limit along the x-axis.

Another example involving a limit at infinity.

```
limit((x + 1/y), {x = 0, y = infinity});
```
This is

$$\lim_{(x,y)\to(0,\infty)} x + \frac{1}{y}$$

The limit is 0.

3.4   Writing a Project Report

You may be assigned a project that involves writing up a Maple investigation or project. You can use the Maple environment to do this. For example, suppose you were asked to write up the ladder investigation you did earlier in this chapter. First, open a new worksheet. You may still have the commands you entered on your current worksheet. If so, you should copy them to the new worksheet and delete the output using the Remove Output item of the Edit menu. Otherwise, type in the following commands from that investigation.

```
[ > ladder:=sqrt((x+a)^2+(y+b)^2);
[ > y/a=b/x;
[ > solve(",y);
[ > ladder:=subs(y=",ladder);
[ > diff(ladder,x);
[ > simplify(");
[ > solve(numer(")=0,x);
[ > diff(ladder,x$2);
[ > simplify(");
```

Insert blank lines before each command.

To do this, move to the end of each line and press the **[>** icon (Maple prompt) on the Tool bar. To place a blank line before the first command, move the cursor between the **[** and **>** on the first line and press the **[>** icon. Your screen should contain something like this:

```
[ >
[ > ladder:=sqrt((x+a)^2+(y+b)^2);
[ >
[ > y/a=b/x;
[ >
[ > solve(",y);
[ >
[ > ladder:=subs(y=",ladder);
[ >
[ > diff(ladder,x);
[ >
[ > simplify(");
[ >
[ > solve(numer(")=0,x);
[ >
```

```
[ > diff(ladder,x$2);
[ >
[ > simplify(");
```

Entering text for your report.

To enter text in a Maple worksheet for your report, move to the blank line at the top of the screen using the mouse or arrow keys. Press the **T** icon in the Tool bar and then type in the desired text. You should insert text for each of the commands following this procedure.

The first six lines of your report might look like this.

```
[   The Ladder Problem:   A Report
The ladder variable is set to
sqrt((x+a)^2+(y+b)^2), the length
of the ladder.
[ > ladder:=sqrt((x+a)^2+(y+b)^2);
[   The ratio of the sides gives us a
relationship between x and y.
[ > y/a=b/x;
```

Making text into a headline.

To make the words "The Ladder Problem: A Report" into a headline, highlight these words and click on the droplist menu on the left of the line under the Tool bar.

Notice that the highlighted words are made larger and boldface.

Converting text to a math expression.

To convert the text "sqrt((x+a)^2+(y+b)^2)" to a math expression, highlight this text and select the the Math Expression item under the Convert to item from the Format menu.

Notice that a square root symbol appears.

Your screen should look something like this when you have completed entering the text to go along with the commands of your report:

```
[   The Ladder Problem: A Report
The ladder variable is set to
```
$$\sqrt{(x + a)\hat{}2 + (y + b)\hat{}2},$$
```
the length  of the ladder.
[ > ladder:=sqrt((x+a)^2+(y+b)^2);
[   The ratio of the sides gives us a
relationship  between x and y.
[ > y/a=b/x;
```

The commands in this report can be executed by simply moving to the first Maple command and pressing Enter once for each command line in the report.

A complete report with output appears at the end of this chapter.

Extensions

Maple Calculus Commands

You can differentiate, integrate, and take limits of functions of one or more variables using the **diff**, **int**, and **limit** commands in Maple. The **simplify** command is often useful in displaying results in a more readable form. The **plot** command can be used to obtain graphic information about a function. This graphic information in conjunction with the first and second derivatives and the **fsolve** command can be useful in investigating the behavior of a function.

Infinite sums can be investigated using the **sum** command. Taylor series can be obtained using the **taylor** command.

The **student** Package

You can load the **student** package for calculus using the **with** command. You can use the **intparts** command in this package to become familiar with the integration by parts technique.

The **student** package contains a variety of commands useful in a calculus course. The **student** package commands allow you to work through the details of a solution to a problem but not to solve the problem directly. The **Int** command sets up an integral that can then be manipulated with such commands as **intparts**, **changevar**, and **powsubs** to reformulate the original integral into a recognizable form. The **powsubs** command substitutes one expression for another in a given expression and is used in trig substitutions in integrals. The **value** command evaluates unevaluated expressions.

Additional Activities

Explore the following functions, making use of the **diff**, **int**, **limit**, **plot**, **simplify**, **fsolve**, **numer**, **denom**, and **taylor** commands.

Accurately locate any maximum and minimum values and points of inflection, and draw a careful sketch of each of the following functions:

1. $f(x) = x^{2/3} - \dfrac{1}{5}x^{5/3}$

2. $f(x) = \dfrac{x^2 + x - 2}{x^2}$

3. $f(x) = \dfrac{\sqrt[3]{1 - x}}{1 + x^2}$

Evaluate the following limits:

4. $\displaystyle\lim_{x\to\infty} \dfrac{2x^2 - 1}{x^2 + 3}$

5. $\displaystyle\lim_{x\to-1} \dfrac{x^2 - 2x + 1}{2x^2 - x - 3}$

6. $\displaystyle\lim_{(x,y)\to(1,3)} x + y^2$

7. $\displaystyle\lim_{(x,y)\to(2,1)} \dfrac{xy - y}{2x + 1}$

Perform the following integrations:

8. $\displaystyle\int x \ln x \, dx$

9. $\displaystyle\int \dfrac{dx}{\sqrt{x^2 - 4}}$

10. $\displaystyle\int \dfrac{2x^2 + 19x - 45}{x^3 - 2x^2 - 5x + 6} \, dx$

11. $\displaystyle\int \dfrac{dx}{4\sin x - 3\cos x}$

12. $\displaystyle\int e^{-x} \cos x \, dx$

13. $\displaystyle\int_0^1 \int_0^{\sqrt{x}} y e^{x^2} \, dy \, dx$

Find and graph the first five terms of the Taylor series expansion about the indicated value a for each of the following:

14. $\cos x, \quad a = 0$

15. $\sin x, \quad a = 0$

16. $\cos x, \quad a = 1$

17. $x \sin 2x, \quad a = 0$

18. $e^x, \quad a = 0$

For the given functions, show that $\dfrac{\partial^2 f(x, y)}{\partial x \partial y} = \dfrac{\partial^2 f(x, y)}{\partial y \partial x}$.

19. $f(x, y) = x^2 y^3 + \cos x \sin y$

20. $f(x, y) = 2^x y^2$

The Ladder Problem: A Report

The ladder variable is set to $\sqrt{(x+a)^2 + (y+b)^2}$, the length of the ladder.

```
>   ladder:=sqrt((x+a)^2+(y+b)^2);
```

$$ladder := \sqrt{x^2 + 2xa + a^2 + y^2 + 2yb + b^2}$$

The ratio of the sides gives us a relationship between x and y.

```
>   y/a=b/x;
```

$$\frac{y}{a} = \frac{b}{x}$$

We solve this equation for y.

```
>   solve(",y);
```

$$\frac{ba}{x}$$

We substitute this value of y in the ladder expression.

```
>   ladder:=subs(y=",ladder);
```

$$ladder := \sqrt{x^2 + 2xa + a^2 + \frac{b^2 a^2}{x^2} + 2\frac{b^2 a}{x} + b^2}$$

Differentiating this for x, we have the first derivative of the ladder function.

```
>   diff(ladder,x);
```

$$\frac{1}{2} \frac{2x + 2a - 2\frac{b^2 a^2}{x^3} - 2\frac{b^2 a}{x^2}}{\sqrt{x^2 + 2xa + a^2 + \frac{b^2 a^2}{x^2} + 2\frac{b^2 a}{x} + b^2}}$$

We simplify this to get an expression that is easier to analyze.

```
>   simplify(");
```

$$\frac{x^4 + x^3\,a - b^2\,a^2 - b^2\,a\,x}{\sqrt{\dfrac{(x^2 + b^2)(x + a)^2}{x^2}}\;x^3}$$

We can now find the zeros of this derivative by finding the zeros of the numerator.

```
>   solve(numer(")=0,x);
```

$$-a,\ (b^2\,a)^{1/3},\ -\frac{1}{2}(b^2\,a)^{1/3} + \frac{1}{2}I\sqrt{3}\,(b^2\,a)^{1/3},$$

$$-\frac{1}{2}(b^2\,a)^{1/3} - \frac{1}{2}I\sqrt{3}\,(b^2\,a)^{1/3}$$

We now have that the solution is $(ab^2)^{(\frac{1}{3})}$.

```
>   diff(ladder,x$2);
```

$$-\frac{1}{4}\frac{\left(2x + 2a - 2\dfrac{b^2\,a^2}{x^3} - 2\dfrac{b^2\,a}{x^2}\right)^2}{\left(x^2 + 2x\,a + a^2 + \dfrac{b^2\,a^2}{x^2} + 2\dfrac{b^2\,a}{x} + b^2\right)^{3/2}}$$

$$+\frac{1}{2}\frac{2 + 6\dfrac{b^2\,a^2}{x^4} + 4\dfrac{b^2\,a}{x^3}}{\sqrt{x^2 + 2x\,a + a^2 + \dfrac{b^2\,a^2}{x^2} + 2\dfrac{b^2\,a}{x} + b^2}}$$

The second derivative can be simplified.

```
>   simplify(");
```

$$\frac{(x^4 + 4x^3\,a + 3a^2\,x^2 + 2b^2\,a\,x + 2b^2\,a^2)\,b^2}{\sqrt{\dfrac{(x^2 + b^2)(x + a)^2}{x^2}}\;x^4\,(x^2 + b^2)}$$

The second derivative seems to be always positive because every term in the numerator is an even power or otherwise positive.

CHAPTER FOUR
Linear Algebra

The linear algebra package, called **linalg**, contains all the standard basic functions of linear algebra, together with a number of special-purpose commands. The first order of business is to load the **linalg** package. This has to be done once at the beginning of each session or if all variables are cleared (possible with some versions but not others).

4.1 The **linalg** Package

*You use the **with** command to load the package.*

```
with(linalg);
```
The names of the commands and functions that are loaded are listed on the screen. Don't be surprised if you are unfamiliar with many of them; linear algebra has been around for a long time and it has many specialized functions.

The Help system covers the new commands in the package.

```
?linalg
```
You can use Maple's Help system at any time to remind yourself of the names of the **linalg** commands or to get help on their use. Alternately, you can call up the Help system with the **help** command, as in **help(linalg)**.

4.2 Matrices and Vectors

In computer science, matrices are also called arrays. In Maple, a matrix is a two-dimensional array with entries indexed by two subscripts, as in $M = \begin{bmatrix} m_{11} & m_{12} \\ m_{21} & m_{22} \end{bmatrix}$. One-dimensional arrays are called *vectors* in Maple; the entries of a vector are indexed by a single subscript, as in $\mathbf{v} = (v_1, v_2)$.

You enter a matrix with the **matrix** *command.*

```
M:=matrix([
[1/2,2/3,3/4,4/5],
[5/6,6/7,7/7,8/9],
[9/10,10/11,11/12,12/13]
]);
```

In Maple, a bracketed sequence [...] of entries is a *list*. Here, the argument to the matrix command is a *list*, the entries of which are also lists. The inside lists are the rows of the matrix, in order. For example, the second row of the matrix M has entries 5/6, 6/7, 7/7, 8/9. You will encounter other forms of the **matrix** command later; this one is the *list-of-lists* form.

If you enter a matrix name, Maple simply echoes the name.

```
M;
```

Maple treats matrix names and function names analogously; when you enter the name of a matrix or function, the definition is not displayed.

You use the **evalm** *command to print the matrix in standard rectangular form.*

```
evalm(M);
```

Think of **evalm** as meaning "evaluate to a matrix."

You can also access the individual entries of the matrix.

```
M[2,3];
```

This returns the entry in the second row and third column. Notice that square brackets are used here, whereas parentheses are used for functions. The notation $M[i, j]$ is "computer subscript notation." Some texts use M_{ij} for the (i, j)-entry of M; others denote it by m_{ij}. Maple uses $M[i, j]$.

You can edit a matrix by reassigning its entries.

```
M[2,3]:=7/8;
```

Here the (2, 3)-entry of the matrix M is changed to 7/8. You might wish to verify the change to M with the **evalm** command. If a matrix has only one row or column, it may appear one-dimensional, but in Maple it is still necessary to address the entries with two subscripts.

Consider the row and column matrices R and C.

```
R:=matrix([[1,2,3,4]]);
C:=matrix([[4],[3],[1],[1]]);
```

Both *R* and *C* appear one-dimensional but, as they are matrices, they are two-dimensional.

You have to use two subscripts to address the entries of any matrix—even one that appears one-dimensional.

```
C[1];
R[1];
```

Some texts use only one subscript to address the entries of row and column matrices; the error messages generated here demonstrate that Maple does not.

*Use the **vector** command to generate an array in which the entries are addressed by a single subscript.*

```
v:=vector([4,3,1,1]);
v[3];
```

In this case, the argument to vector is a single list. Note that Maple does not consider **v** to be a matrix; the data structure **v** is perhaps best thought of as the ordered 4-tuple $\mathbf{v} = (v[1], v[2], v[3], v[4])$.

Maple is consistent in its response to array names.

```
v;
```

Consistency is a virtue.

You edit vectors, like matrices, by reassigning the components.

```
v[3]:=2;
```

Modifying the components of a one-dimensional array is analogous to modifying the entries of a two-dimensional array, except that only one index is used.

*The **evalm** command works for vectors as it does for matrices.*

```
evalm(v);
```

Note that Maple prints the vector with commas between its entries; but matrices of modest width are not printed with commas.

Solving Systems of Linear Equations

Solving systems of linear equations is a straightforward but time-consuming, error-prone task for which Maple is well equipped. You have already used the **solve** command in Chapter 2. You can use the **solve** command to solve any system of equations. Here is a typical system of linear equations.

$$\begin{cases} 3x_2 - 4x_3 + \frac{5}{3}x_4 = \frac{23}{12} \\ 2x_1 + 7x_2 + \frac{4}{3}x_3 + 3x_4 = \frac{41}{4} \\ \frac{1}{2}x_1 - 3x_2 + 2x_3 + \frac{13}{3}x_4 = \frac{41}{12} \\ \frac{7}{6}x_1 + \frac{7}{3}x_2 - \frac{14}{9}x_3 + 7x_4 = \frac{35}{4} \end{cases}$$

This enters the system into the session.

```
Sys:=
{3*x2-4*x3+5/3*x4=23/12,
2*x1+7*x2+4/3*x3+3*x4=41/4,
1/2*x1-3*x2+2*x3+13/3*x4=41/12,
7/6*x1+7/3*x2-14/9*x3+7*x4=35/4};
```

Note that commas are used to separate the equations and that the sequence of equations is enclosed in set braces.

You can now use **solve** *to find the solutions.*

```
solve(Sys,{x1,x2,x3,x4});
```

Maple reports all solutions that it finds—in this case, all that exist.

Notice that $x1$, $x2$, $x3$, $x4$ are used here rather than $x[1]$, $x[2]$, $x[3]$, $x[4]$. This style of "subscripting" seems more natural in some circumstances, but either style can be used.

You may find that you prefer to solve a linear system by using Gaussian elimination on the augmented matrix of the system.

```
AM:=
matrix([
[0,3,-4,5/3,23/12],
[2,7,4/3,3,41/4],
[1/2,-3,2,13/3,41/12],
[7/6,7/3,-14/9,7,35/4]
]);
```

Entering the augmented matrix of the system requires significantly fewer keystrokes than entering the equations.

If you like, you can step through the Gaussian elimination procedure using the Maple commands **swaprow**, **mulrow**, and **addrow**.

You use **swaprow** *to interchange the order of two rows.*

```
SR:=swaprow(AM,1,2);
```

Note that the matrix name is the first argument to the command, followed by the numbers of the rows to be swapped.

You use **mulrow** *to multiply a scalar times a row.*

```
MR:=mulrow(SR,1,1/2);
```

The matrix name comes first, then the number of the row to be multiplied, and then the multiplier.

You use **addrow** *to add a multiple of one row to another row.*

```
AR:=addrow(MR,1,3,-1/2);
```

Again, the first argument is the matrix name and the second argument is the number of the row to be multiplied; this is then followed by the number of the row to which the multiple is to be added, and then by the multiplier.

Alternately, you can partially automate the reduction by using **pivot** *in place of* **addrow**.

```
pivot(AR,2,2);
```

The **pivot** command uses **addrow** to zero the entries above and below the specified entry. Here, the (2, 2)-entry is specified. You can also limit the pivot operation to forward or backward pivoting. Use **?pivot** for more details.

Maple also provides several automated procedures for Gaussian elimination. A few restrictions are placed on these routines; they work for matrices with entries that are quotients of polynomial expressions with rational coefficients, but they will not work on matrices that contain, for example, square roots that are not rational. For such matrices with more general entries, you will have to fall back on manual row reduction with **addrow**, **mulrow**, **swaprow**, and **pivot**.

The **gausselim** *routine uses elementary row operations to do forward elimination.*

```
GE:=gausselim(AM);
```
The first nonzero entry of each row of the result is frequently called the pivotal entry. Note that the entries above the pivotal entries have not been zeroed.

Alternately, you can do fraction-free forward Gaussian elimination.

```
FF:=ffgausselim(AM);
```
As its name suggests, the **ffgausselim** command performs Gaussian elimination without introducing any fractions.

You can take the matrix AM all the way to reduced row echelon form with the **gaussjord** *command.*

```
RR:=gaussjord(AM);
```
The **gaussjord** command performs standard Gauss-Jordan elimination on the matrix to produce the reduced row echelon form.

Alternately, you can use the command **rref** *as a synonym for* **gaussjord***.*

```
rref(AM);
```
You may prefer **rref** to **gaussjord** for its brevity. Of course, **rref** is an abbreviation of "reduced row echelon form."

The reduced row echelon form is preferred by many because it is unique and it makes the back substitution trivial. However, numerical analysts frequently prefer to do only forward elimination (as is done with the **gausselim** routine) and then perform back substitution.

Although it is a fairly simple matter to complete the solution of the original system by back substitution using any of the matrices *GE*, *FF*, or *RR*, you may choose to have Maple do it for you. This is especially handy for larger systems, where back substitution can become quite time consuming.

Use **backsub** *to automate back substitution.*

```
backsub(FF);
```
The **backsub** command will work on any matrix in echelon form. Each of the routines **gausselim**, **ffgausselim**, and **rref** (**gaussjord**) leaves the matrix in a form suitable for **backsub**.

Note that the solution produced by **backsub** is completely general; all solutions are produced by varying the parameter that appears in the solution.

Sometimes you may need to solve several systems with the same coefficient matrix. This is a situation that occurs frequently in applications. For example, assume you need to solve the system **Sys**, with which you have been working, for each of a variety of "right-hand sides," including $c[1] = (23/12, 41/4, 41/12, 35/4)$, $c[2] = (5, 0, -13/4, 7/4)$, and so on. The augmented matrix, *AM*, of the first system has already been entered and the first system solved. An analogous procedure would suffice for the remaining systems. But if you think of *AM* as the matrix *K* of coefficients of the unknowns, augmented by the column **c** of right-hand sides, then it would clearly be more efficient to extract *K* and reuse it with **c**[2], and so on. Maple has block-editing commands that allow you to do this.

You can extract the coefficient matrix from AM with the **submatrix** *command.*

```
K:=submatrix(AM,1..4,1..4);
```
The first argument to the **submatrix** command is the matrix name, followed by the row range and then the column range.

Augment K by each of the new right-hand sides, in turn, and then proceed as before.

```
c[2]:=vector([5,0,-13/4,7/4]);
AM:=augment(K,c[2]);
gausselim(AM);
backsub(");
```
Notice that here, **c**[2] is used as a name for a vector. The *i*th component of **c**[2] is **c**[2][*i*]. The use of this notation implicitly defines **c** as a *table*. Tables are related to arrays but are more general. The command **print(c)** will display the table. You can use **?table** for more information on tables.

You can determine all vectors **g** *for which the system is consistent.*

```
g:=vector([g1,g2,g3,g4]);
AM:=augment(K,g);
GE:=gausselim(AM,4);
```
The second argument to **gausselim** (4 in this case) stops the **gausselim** procedure from using pivots to the right of the specified column; this ensures that entries that are conditionally zero are not used as pivots.

In this case, the system is consistent if, and only if, the (4, 5)-entry of GE is 0.

```
g[1]:=solve(GE[4,5]=0,g1);
```
Clearly, setting $GE[4, 5] = 0$ is equivalent to letting **g**[1] be the solution of the equation $GE[4, 5] = 0$.

The general solution vector is now **g**.

```
evalm(g);
```
Any vector **v** for which the linear system with augmented matrix $[K, \mathbf{v}]$ is consistent is now of the same form as **g**: **v**[2], **v**[3], and **v**[4] are arbitrary and **v**[1] = **v**[4] − 1/3 **v**[2] − **v**[3].

Proceeding as before, you can find the solution of the general (solvable) system.

```
AM:=augment(K,g);
GE:=gausselim(AM,4);
```

Complete the process with **backsub**.

```
backsub(");
```
The vector returned gives a formula for the coefficients of the solution.

Additional Editing Commands

It is quite convenient at times to be able to use just part of a matrix, or to piece vectors and matrices together to form new matrices, as when several linear systems with the same coefficient matrix are to be solved. In addition to the **submatrix** and **augment** commands, Maple provides several other useful "editing tools." With the **submatrix** command, you specify the range of rows and columns you want to keep. To keep one row or column, it may be easier to use the **row** or **col** commands.

Use the **row** *command to pick out a single row.*

```
r:=row(AM,3);
```
The **row** command returns a vector—in this case, the third row of *AM*.

Use the **col** *command to pick out a single column.*

```
c:=col(AM,5);
```
The **col** command also returns a vector—in this case, the fifth column of *AM*.

Sometimes you may prefer to specify a range of rows or columns you want to delete. You can do this with the **delrows** and **delcols** commands.

Use **delrows** *or* **delcols** *to delete rows or columns.*

```
delcols(AM,5..5);
```
The first argument to **delcols** is the name of the matrix; the second argument is the range of columns to be deleted. Notice that this is equivalent to the less compact command **submatrix(AM,1..4,1..4)**. The **delrows** command works analogously to delete rows.

*The **stack** command allows vertical augmentation.*

```
stack(K,c,v);
```

Both **augment** and **stack** will accept any number of arguments. The arguments can be matrices or vectors or any combination thereof. The lengths of the vectors must all be the same and (for **stack**) equal to the width of any matrix arguments.

An Important Point on Names

On some occasions, it may be convenient to make a copy of an existing array and change a few of the entries. Here, you can use the **copy** command.

*Use **copy** to make a copy of an array.*

```
cc:=copy(c);
cc[1]:=0;
cc[1];
c[1];
```

Note that *c*[1] is unchanged. In this case, *cc* is not the same matrix as *c*.

*The result is quite different if the **copy** command is not used.*

```
cc:=c;
cc[1]:=0;
c[1];
```

In this case, *cc* and *c* are two names for the same matrix.

Summary and Extensions

You use the **matrix** command to enter a matrix, as in

$$A := matrix([[1,2],[3,4]])$$

You use the **vector** command to enter a vector, as in

$$v := vector([1, 2, 3, 4])$$

It is best to think of vectors as *n*-tuples in Maple. In particular, vectors are not matrices. The (*i*, *j*)-entry of a matrix *A* is denoted *A*[*i*, *j*]. The *i*th entry of a vector **v** is denoted **v**[*i*]. You use the assignment operator (**:=**) to change an entry of a matrix or vector. The command **A[2,3]:=4** assigns the value 4 to the (2, 3)-entry of a matrix *A*. The command **v[2]:=3** assigns the value 3 to the second component of **v**. You use **evalm(E)** to have Maple evaluate and display the entries of a matrix or vector expression *E*.

Systems of linear equations can be solved by row-reducing the augmented matrix of the system and applying **backsub**. The row reduction can be done step by step with **addrow**, **mulrow**, and **swaprow**, or automated with **gausselim**, **ffgausselim**, or **gaussjord** (**rref**). Alternately, you can partially automate the reduction with **pivot**.

Maple provides several editing commands for matrices. The **augment**, **stack**, **submatrix**, **delrows**, and **delcols** commands allow easy cutting and pasting of parts of matrices.

Related Commands   (use the Help facility (**?**) for further information): **copyinto**, **minor**, **subvector**.

Additional Activities

1. Enter the 4×6 matrix $A = [a_{ij}]$, where each entry is defined by $a_{ij} = i/(i + j)$.

2. Use **gausselim** and **backsub** to solve the linear system having the matrix A of Activity 1 as its augmented matrix.

3. Use the **delcols** and **augment** commands to replace the sixth column of the matrix A of Activity 1 by the vector $\mathbf{v} = (v_i) \in R^4$ defined by $v_i = i^{32}$; save the result as B.

4. Use **gausselim** and **backsub** to solve the linear system having the matrix B of Activity 3 as its augmented matrix.

5. Solve the following linear system by using row reduction and back substitution on its augmented matrix:

$$\begin{cases} 2x_1 + 3x_2 + 4x_3 + 5x_4 + 6x_5 + 7x_6 = 8 \\ 3x_1 + 3x_2 + 4x_3 + 5x_4 + 6x_5 + 7x_6 = 11 \\ 4x_1 + 4x_2 + 4x_3 + 5x_4 + 6x_5 + 7x_6 = 37 \\ 5x_1 + 5x_2 + 5x_3 + 5x_4 + 6x_5 + 7x_6 = 32 \end{cases}$$

6. Use **ffgausselim** and **backsub** to show that, if $a \neq b$, then, for every x, the linear system with the following augmented matrix is consistent:

$$M = \begin{bmatrix} a & b & x \\ a+1 & b+1 & x+1 \\ a+2 & b+2 & x+2 \\ a+3 & b+3 & x+3 \\ a+4 & b+4 & x+4 \\ a+5 & b+5 & x+5 \\ a+6 & b+6 & x+6 \\ a+7 & b+7 & x+7 \\ a+8 & b+8 & x+8 \\ a+9 & b+9 & x+9 \end{bmatrix}$$

4.3 More on Matrices and Vectors

Matrix and Vector Arithmetic

The same arithmetic operation symbols are used on matrices as are used on numbers, except that the compound symbol "ampersand-star" (`&*`) is used for matrix multiplication and the **innerprod** command is used for matrix-vector and vector-matrix multiplication. The "star" symbol (`*`) is reserved for scalar multiplication. The **evalm** command is applied to vector and matrix expressions to instruct Maple to evaluate them.

First things first.

```
with(linalg);
```

One approach to matrix-vector arithmetic is to build the expression to be evaluated and then apply the **evalm** command. You build an arithmetic matrix expression as you would any arithmetic expression, using `&*` for matrix products.

Consider the two matrices A and M given here, for example.

```
A:=matrix([
[0,3,-4,5],
[2,7,4/3,9],
[1/2,-3,2,13],
[4/3,7,-2/3,11/3]]);
M:=matrix([
[1,2],
[3,4],
[2,3],
[4,5]]);
```

The matrices can be entered all on one line or split at any convenient point.

Define the expression S from A and M.

```
S:=A &* M;
```

Note that *S* is not evaluated. The spaces around **&*** are for emphasis in this first use of the symbol; spaces are not required in general, except that a space is required between **&*** and **"**.

You can use expressions in defining other expressions.

```
F:=A^2&*(2*M-S-M);
```

Note that the definition of *F* uses *S*.

*Use **evalm** to get the evaluated form of the result.*

```
evalm(F);
```

The result is given in standard rectangular form.

*It is also possible to "wrap" expressions with **evalm**, using standard function notation.*

```
evalm(A&*M+S);
```

Sometimes you may want to manipulate an expression before calling **evalm**. At other times, you may just want the detailed answer straightaway. You will develop your own preferred style with **evalm**. Think of it as a "button" you push when you want to see the answer in full matrix form.

*You can use **print** to review the definition of an expression.*

```
print(F);
```

The **print** command does not cause a matrix expression involving arithmetic operators to be evaluated. (Some simplification may be performed.)

*Following standard convention, Maple sometimes uses **0** to denote the zero matrix.*

```
A-A;
```

When Maple returns the symbol **0** for the zero matrix, there is no way to determine the dimensions of the matrix except to look back at the dimensions of the matrices that produced the result. However, typically the answer gives all the information that is required.

You can treat a scalar as a scalar matrix for addition.

```
evalm(A+3);
```

Note that the scalar has been treated as if it were the matrix $S = [s_{ij}]$ of the same size as *M* with

$$s_{ij} = \begin{cases} 3 & \text{if } i = j \\ 0 & \text{if } i \neq j \end{cases}$$

You cannot, however, treat a scalar as a scalar matrix for multiplication.

```
evalm(3&*A);
```

Maple insists that ***** be used for multiplication by scalars.

*One seeming exception to this rule is that **0** can be used with **&***.*

```
evalm(0&*A);
```

This is consistent with Maple's use of **0** as the zero matrix.

In most cases, you cannot use the scalar multiplication operator for matrix multiplication. A useful exception is for powers.	`B:=evalm(A*A);` Maple evaluates products that use ***** without regard to the order of the terms. Because matrix multiplication is highly noncommutative, the designers of Maple have taken a conservative approach to allowing ***** for matrix products. However, order is not a problem for powers.
Maple can be very particular about the use of ***** *and* **&*** *.*	`evalm(M&*3*S);` In this case, Maple uses left-to-right evaluation because **&*** and ***** have the same precedence. Because **M&*3** is an illegal expression, an error message results. Either use **evalm(M &*(3*S))** or relocate the scalar.

Vector addition and scalar multiplication are similar to the corresponding matrix operations.	`v:=vector([-143/3,-47,-99/2,-31]);`
	`evalm(2*v-k*v);`
	Here, *k* acts as a symbolic scalar because it has not been assigned a value.

You can use an array without naming it.	`evalm(v+vector([3,7,-2/3,6]));` Matrices can be used in the same "on the fly" manner.
You can add a scalar to a vector, but the result is not analogous to adding it to a matrix.	`w:=evalm(v+3);` Here, the scalar has been treated as if it were the vector **s** = (3, 3, 3, 3). Compare this result to the calculation of *M* + 3 above.

You can multiply matrices and vectors, in either order, using the **innerprod** *command. The result is a vector.*	`innerprod(A,w);`
	`innerprod(v,A);`
	In the first case, **w** is treated as if it were a column. In the second case, **v** is treated as if it were a row. This is a common extension to the definition of matrix multiplication.

You can use **innerprod** *with a vector on either end (or both or neither) and one or more matrices in the middle.*	`innerprod(v,A,B,w);` Here, **v** is treated as if it were a row and **w** is treated as if it were a column. Of course, the computation will fail if the arrays are not of appropriate sizes to be multiplied—the length of **v** must agree with the height of *A*, the width of *A* with the height of *B*, and the width of *B* with the length of **w**. In this case, the result is a scalar.
The ampersand-star operation can also be used to compute the product **Aw** *of a matrix times a vector if the vector is on the right-hand side.*	`evalm(A&*w);` Vectors are treated as columns by the ampersand-star operation. The result is the same as **innerprod(A,w)**.

*However, you cannot compute the product **v**A using the ampersand-star operation.*

```
evalm(v&*A);
```
Vectors can be used only on the right side of the **&*** operation.

*You can use the rather unappealing compound symbol **&*( )** for the identity matrix. But you might wish to **alias** it to something else.*

```
alias(ID=&*());
evalm(ID&*A);
```
In this way you can choose pretty much any name you wish for the identity. Notice that whenever you use the **alias** command, it returns a complete list of all the aliases in effect.

*If you add the identity to another matrix, the effect is the same as adding the scalar **1**.*

```
evalm(A+ID);
evalm(A+1);
```
The symbol **I** is initially aliased to the complex number *i*. Changing it simply causes Maple to respond $(-1)^{1/2}$ when it would have responded with **I**, but you might prefer to use an alternate symbol, perhaps **ID**, for the identity matrix.

Other Forms of the Matrix and Vector Commands

Maple provides several alternative forms of the **matrix** and **vector** commands that you may find preferable in some cases. The **matrix** command can be used in the form

```
matrix(m,n,spec)
```

where **m** and **n** are the number of rows and columns and **spec** is either a list of lists, or a list of entries, or a vector or a function of two variables. The **vector** command can be used in the form

```
vector(m,spec)
```

where **m** is the number of entries and **spec** is either a list or a function of one variable.

*You can specify m and n with the list-of-lists form of the **matrix** command, if you wish.*

```
M:=matrix(2,3,[[1,2,3],[2,3,4]]);
```
As you now know, the specification of *m* and *n* is optional in this case.

*You have similar latitude with the **vector** command.*

```
v:=vector(3,[1,2,3]);
```
The specification of *m* is optional.

If you supply m and n, the third argument to the **matrix** *command can be a simple list, rather than a list of lists.*	```L:=matrix(4,2,[1,2,3,4,5,6,7,8]);``` This is the *list form* of the **matrix** command. When the matrix is formed, the list is broken into four groups of two entries. Many people prefer this form over the list-of-lists form for ease of data entry; others feel it lacks some of the naturalness of the list-of-lists form.
Although a vector is not just a list, Maple will let you treat it as one in this one case.	```V:=matrix(3,1,v);``` This facility provides an easy way to convert a vector to a matrix. The order of the indices determines whether the result will be a row or a column. Type **?matrix** for a complete description of the use of vectors with **matrix**.
The third argument to the **matrix** *command can also be a function of two variables.*	```M:=matrix(7,9,(i,j) -> i/j);``` This is the function form of the **matrix** command. The third argument can be any function of two variables. In this case, the (i, j)-entry will be i/j. This is usually the quickest form to use when it is applicable.
Named functions, either built-in or user-defined, provide particularly easy matrix entry.	```Z:=matrix(3,3,0);``` For any rational number r, the function $x \rightarrow r$ is called r in Maple. Many texts use this convention for all numbers, but Maple uses it only for rationals.
You can use the **0** *function and "generic identity matrix"* **ID** *to define identity matrices of a particular size.*	```Ident[9]:=evalm(matrix(9,9,0)+ID);``` Recall that **ID** is aliased to **&*( )**. Because it is so easy to create an identity matrix of any desired specific size, Maple does not have an identity matrix function. Note that the notation *ID*[9] cannot be used here—it would conflict with the aliasing of *ID*.
You can also use a function form of the **vector** *command.*	```v:=vector(20,i->i^2);``` Here, the function is a function of only one variable. The result contains the squares of the first 20 natural numbers.
Diagonal matrices are easy to enter with the **diag** *command.*	```diag(1,5,2,4,3);``` This saves a lot of time over any other way of entering diagonal matrices.
The **diag** *command also accepts square matrices as arguments.*	```diag(Z,1,2,matrix(3,3,1));``` The result is what is called a *block diagonal matrix*. Note that **diag** is a synonym for **BlockDiagonal**. Both commands accept either "scalars" or square matrices as arguments.

*If you specify m and n with the **matrix** command, the third argument can also be omitted completely. The result is a symbolic matrix.*

```
S:=matrix(3,3);
evalm(S);
```

The (i, j)-entry of S is simply $S[i, j]$. Symbolic matrices are useful for general verification of matrix properties.

This creates a symbolic vector.

```
s:=vector(5);
evalm(s);
```

The ith component of **s** is **s**$[i]$.

If you want to test an idea on numerical matrices, Maple will generate examples for you.

You can generate random integer matrices.

```
R:=randmatrix(20,20);
```

This generates a pseudorandom 20×20 matrix of integers.

*You can test a hypothesis on a large matrix generated with the **sparse** option.*

```
RS:=randmatrix(30,15,sparse);
```

The **sparse** option causes the matrix to have a lot of zero entries.

A Note on Arrays, Loops, and Sequences

The loop is one of the most useful utilities in computing. In particular, loops are a great convenience for automating repetitive tasks. The principal form of the loop in Maple is

for *count* **from** *start* **by** *inc* **to** *finish*
  do
    stufftodo
  od;

where *count* is a variable, *start* and *finish* are the beginning and ending values of *count*, and *inc* is the amount by which *count* is to be incremented on each repetition. The thing(s) to be done are listed between the **do** and **od** (and separated by semicolons if there is more than one). The "from clause" or "by clause" are optional; if omitted, the default values of *start* or *inc* are 1. Hence, "**for i to 3 do ... od**" is equivalent to "**for i from 1 by 1 to 3 do ... od**." The variable *count* can be an assigned or unassigned variable; in either case, it has the value *finish* + 1 after the execution of the loop.

You can use loops to edit vectors or matrices.

```
v:=vector(27,i->1);
for i from 1 by 2 to 27
  do
    v[i]:=0
  od;
```

All entries of **v** with odd subscripts are changed to 0.

This verifies the change.

```
evalm(v);
```

Loops are also convenient for defining a collection of related structures.

```
for i from 1 to 9
  do
    v[i]:=vector(5,j -> j/i)
  od;
```

The counter retains a value after the execution of the loop.

```
i;
```

The fact that **i** has a value will cause no problems if you reuse it in a loop (the loop will reset it), but it might cause unpleasant surprises in other uses of **i**.

*Note that Maple distinguishes between **i** and **'i'**.*

```
'i';
```

The value of **'i'** is the original, unassigned value of **i**—not the value assigned to **i**.

*If you have no need for **i** to retain its present assignment, it is best to unassign it.*

```
i:='i';
```

This has the effect of unassigning **i**. Note that you use regular (forward) quotes and not back quotes here.

Summary

The **matrix** command has a variety of forms. The list form of the **matrix** command is generally quicker to use than the list-of-lists form. However, both forms have their proponents. The function forms of the **matrix** and **vector** commands are probably the most efficient to use when they are applicable.

Symbolic matrices and vectors provide a means of verifying properties in general for low dimensions.

The **randmatrix** command generates pseudorandom matrices, which are helpful for checking conjectures. It is generally much quicker to do a calculation with randomly generated numerical matrices than with symbolic matrices. Hence, **randmatrix** provides an attractive way to test hypotheses.

You can use the **diag** command to enter diagonal (or block diagonal) matrices more easily.

You can use the **innerprod** command to compute the product of a matrix and a vector, a vector and a matrix, a vector and a vector, or a matrix and a matrix.

Related Commands **array, BlockDiagonal, companion.**

Additional Activities

1. Enter the 5×8 matrix A for which the (i, j)-entry is the quotient $i/(i + j)$.

2. Find a function form for the definition of the matrix

$$A = \begin{bmatrix} 1 & 2 & 3 & 4 \\ 2 & 3 & 4 & 5 \\ 3 & 4 & 5 & 6 \\ 4 & 5 & 6 & 7 \\ 5 & 6 & 7 & 8 \end{bmatrix}$$

3. Create the matrix

$$B = \begin{bmatrix} 1 & 2 \\ 2 & 3 \\ 4 & 5 \end{bmatrix}$$

by using the **submatrix** command on the matrix A of Activity 2.

4. Repeat Activity 3 using the **delrows** and **delcols** commands.

5. Use the function form of the **vector** command to enter the vector $\mathbf{v}$ in R^{20} with ith entry $\mathbf{i}^3$.

6. Use the function form of the **matrix** command to enter the 10×10 matrix $I_{10} = [\delta_{ij}]$, where

$$\delta_{ij} = \begin{cases} 1 & \text{if } i = j \\ 0 & \text{if } i \neq j \end{cases}$$

Let M be a random 10×10 matrix, and let A be the augmented matrix $[M, I_{10}]$. Row-reduce A to reduced row echelon form $F = [L, R]$, and verify that the right-hand side R of F satisfies $RM = L$. Note that L is the reduced row echelon form of M.

7. Use **augment** and **rref** to show that every vector **x** in R^{10} is a multiple of the 10×10 matrix $M = [m_{ij}]$ defined by $m_{ij} = \min(i, j)$.

8. Verify that the matrix

$$A = \begin{bmatrix} 1 & 2 & 3 & 4 \\ 2 & 3 & 4 & 5 \\ 3 & 4 & 5 & 6 \\ 4 & 5 & 6 & 7 \end{bmatrix}$$

satisfies the equation $A\mathbf{v} = (x, x + 1, x + 2, x + 3)$, for every vector $\mathbf{v} = (s + 2t - x + 2, -2s - 3t + x - 1, s, t)$.

9. Let

$$B = \begin{bmatrix} 1 & 2 & 3 & 4 & 5 \\ 2 & 3 & 4 & 5 & 1 \\ 3 & 4 & 5 & 1 & 2 \\ 4 & 5 & 1 & 2 & 3 \\ 5 & 1 & 2 & 3 & 4 \end{bmatrix}$$

Evaluate the "matrix polynomial" $B^5 - 15B^4 - 25B^3 + 375B^2 + 125B - 1875$.

4.4 Basic Matrix and Vector Functions

The standard basic matrix and vector functions and commands are contained in the **linalg** package. In this section, you will see how they are used in the Maple environment.

At least you only have to do this once per session.

```
with(linalg);
alias(ID=&*());
```

If, during a session, you find that Maple seems to not understand **linalg** commands, try a simple command like **matrix(1,1)**. If you have loaded the **linalg** package, Maple should respond **[?[1,1]]**. If Maple responds instead with **matrix(1,1)**, you probably have forgotten to load the **linalg** package. If loading **linalg** cures this problem, you may have to redefine any matrices or vectors you entered before loading the package.

You can compute the determinant of a matrix.

```
Max:=matrix(5,5,(i,j)->max(i,j));
det(Max);
```

You can compute the adjoint of a matrix—not a favorite pastime for many when done by hand.

```
Adj:=adjoint(Max);
```
The calculation of the adjoint of a 5×5 matrix requires the calculation of the determinants of 25 4×4 matrices.

*If you wish to investigate the properties of a function like **det**, you can work with symbolic matrices and vectors.*

```
S:=matrix(2,2);
det(S);
```
This gives the familiar formula for the determinant of a 2×2 matrix. You will not want to do this for matrices much larger than 4×4, however, due to the length of the output. (The formula for the determinant of a 5×5 has 120 terms, each a product of 5 terms; some machines may not have the resources to handle that. Try it.)

You can compute the inverse of an invertible matrix.

```
inverse(Max);
```
This can also be done with either **evalm(Max^(-1))** or **evalm(1/Max)**. The simplicity of the inverse of the matrix *Max* may be bit of a surprise. You might like to experimentally determine a formula for the inverse of the $n \times n$ analogue of *Max*.

*If you apply the **inverse** command to a singular matrix, you get an error message.*

```
M:=matrix(5,5,(i,j)->i+j mod 2);
inverse(M);
```
Some programs return a generalized inverse if the regular inverse does not exist. Maple does not.

You can compute the inverse of a matrix with undefined entries.

```
inverse(S);
```
This gives the familiar formula for the inverse of an invertible 2×2 matrix. Like **det**, the **inverse** command requires substantial resources if used with larger symbolic matrices. Even if your machine has the resources to handle it, chances are you will not want to wait for a formula for the inverse of a 20×20 matrix.

You can check that the product of a matrix and its adjoint is the scalar matrix det(A)I.

```
S:=matrix(4,4);
A:=adjoint(S);
alias(DetS=det(S));
evalm(A&*S);
map(simplify,");
```
Aliasing **DetS** to **det(S)** gives the output in a meaningful form following simplification of the entries. The final command forces the simplification of the entries.

You can use **inverse** *to solve a linear system Mx = y if the coefficient matrix is nonsingular.*

```
y:=vector([6,9,6,9,6]);
evalm(inverse(M)&*y);
```
Of course, this works only if *M* is invertible, which it is not in this case.

Alternately, you can use the **linsolve** *command to solve a linear system Mx = y.*

```
linsolve(M,y);
```
The **linsolve** command is somewhat analogous to multiplication on the left by the inverse, but does not require that the coefficient matrix be invertible.

This solves the linear system *Mx = y* for *x*. In this case, there are many solutions. Notice that if *A* = [*M*, **v**] is the augmented matrix of the system, then **linsolve(M,v)** is analogous to **G:=backsub(gausselim(A))**. However, the solutions from the two procedures will not always have precisely the same form because the procedures use slightly different algorithms. Note that the components of the solution vector can be used to write *y* as a linear combination of the column vectors of *M*.

You can also use **linsolve** *to solve a matrix equation AX = B for X.*

```
B:=augment(y,2*y);
X:=linsolve(M,B);
```
The second argument need not be a column matrix. Notice that the solution has been assigned the name *X*.

You may find the response of **linsolve** *puzzling on occasions.*

```
linsolve(M,Max);
```
All solutions found are reported—in this case, none has been found.

You can compute the transpose of a matrix.

```
transpose(X);
```
As you can see, the rows and columns are interchanged.

The standard vector functions are also available.

You can compute the cross product of vectors in R^3.

```
u:=vector([1,1,1]);
v:=vector([0,1,-1]);
w:=crossprod(u,v);
```
Recall that the cross product of two vectors is orthogonal to both.

You can compute the dot product of vectors.

```
dotprod(u,w);
```
Note that this is the same as **innerprod(v,w)**. In this case, the result verifies that **w** is orthogonal to **v**.

You can compute the norm of a vector.

```
norm(u,2);
```
Mathematicians use a variety of norms on vectors and matrices; this is the standard one, $\|\mathbf{v}\| = \sqrt{\mathbf{v} \cdot \mathbf{v}}$. You might wish to compare the result of this command to the result of the command **norm(v)**

to convince yourself that you must be careful. See the Help page on **norm** for more information.

You can also compute the angle between two vectors.

```
angle(v,w);
```
Recall that the angle θ between two vectors **v** and **w** satisfies $\mathbf{v} \cdot \mathbf{w} = \|\mathbf{u}\| \, \|\mathbf{v}\| \cos(\theta)$.

More on Subscripts and Sequences

Subscripts and sequences are intimately tied together. In Maple, any collection of objects separated by commas forms a *sequence*. Hence, a list is a sequence enclosed in square brackets, a set is a sequence enclosed in curly braces, and so on. Sequences are generated in Maple with the **seq** command. The syntax of the **seq** command resembles that of the definite integral command, **int(f(x),x=1..5)**.

*Here the **seq** command generates an initial segment of the sequence of factorials.*

```
F:=seq(i!,i=0..10);
```
$F[i]$ is now $(i-1)!$.

*The **seq** command also supports the **s1,s2,...**, form of subscripting if you use a dot between the **s** and the **i**.*

```
seq(s.i,i=1..5);
```
The dot (period) is the *concatenation operator* in Maple. (To concatenate two strings of symbols means to put them end to end to form one; hence, **s.3** evaluates to **s3**.)

*You can use the **seq** command effectively to generate an argument for a function of several variables, like **augment**.*

```
S:=matrix(5,5);
seq(row(S,i),i=1..5);
T:=augment(");
```
This builds a new matrix having the rows of S as its columns. Hence, T is the transpose of S.

You can also create the desired sequence manually. Which approach is more efficient depends on the number of terms.

```
row(S,1),
row(S,2),
row(S,3),
row(S,4),
row(S,5);
T:=augment(");
```
Notice the commas between the **row** commands.

Used at the right times, the **seq** command can save a lot of typing.

Polynomials and Matrices: The Cayley-Hamilton Theorem

Polynomials and matrices interact in a number of interesting ways. In this section you will see how Maple can be used to explore one of them.

You can compute the characteristic polynomial $\det(xI - A)$ of a square matrix either directly or using Maple's **charpoly** *command.*

```
A:=matrix(3,3,(i,j)->i+j-1 mod 3);
p:=charpoly(A,x);
```
Note that the characteristic polynomial has degree 3 and constant term $(-1)^3 \det(A)$.

The Cayley-Hamilton theorem, named after its discoverers, says that every square matrix is a root of its own characteristic equation $C_A(x) = 0$.

```
subs(x=A,p);
evalm(");
```
That certainly verifies the Cayley-Hamilton theorem for the matrix A. But isn't it obvious that $\det(AI - A) = 0$? Yes, of course. But the Cayley-Hamilton theorem makes the substitution $x = A$ after taking the determinant. In the first case, the answer is the number 0; in the second case, it is the matrix 0.

You can verify the Cayley-Hamilton theorem in general for low dimensions using Maple's symbolic capabilities.

```
M:=matrix(3,3);
evalm(charpoly(M,M));
```
Perhaps some simplification would help.

Use the **map** *command to cause the specified command to work on the entries of the matrix.*

```
map(simplify,");
```
Most mathematical functions (sin, cos, and so on) are mapped onto the entries of a matrix by the **evalm** command. However, some Maple system commands, like **simplify**, are not; these are handled with the **map** command.

It follows from the Cayley-Hamilton theorem that if p is any polynomial and if r is the remainder on dividing p by the characteristic polynomial of A, then $p(A) = r(A)$. Because the degree of the remainder is always smaller than the degree of the divisor, it follows that no polynomial in A need be written in a form with degree more than 2.

Use the **rem** *command to compute the remainder on dividing one polynomial by another.*

```
rem(x^7-4*x^3+1,x^3-3*x^2-3*x+9,x);
```
Recall that given any two polynomials p and d, p can be written in the form

$$p = qd + r$$

where r is either 0 or has degree less than the degree of d.

The **rem** *command also works on polynomial functions.*

```
p:=x->x^7-4*x^3+1;
r:=x->rem(p(x),charpoly(A,x),x);
```

You can now verify that $p(A) = r(A)$.

```
p(A);
evalm(");
r(A);
evalm(");
```

You might prefer to verify that $p(A) - r(A) = 0$.

Polynomials and Matrices: Curve Fitting

Two points, (x_1, y_1) and (x_2, y_2), with distinct x-coordinates, determine a line and therefore a polynomial of the form $p(x) = ax + b$. Similarly, three points—(x_1, y_1), (x_2, y_2), and (x_3, y_3), with distinct x-coordinates—determine a polynomial of the form $p(x) = a + bx + cx^2$, and so on. Finding the equation of the polynomial

$$p(x) = a_0 + a_1 x + \cdots + a_n x^n$$

determined by $n + 1$ points in the form $(x_1, y_1), (x_2, y_2), \ldots, (x_{n+1}, y_{n+1})$, with distinct x-coordinates, requires solving a system of $n + 1$ equations in $n + 1$ unknowns. The system is generated by evaluating the equation $p(x_i) = y_i$, for $i = 1 \ldots n + 1$. In matrix form, the system is $M\mathbf{a} = \mathbf{y}$, where

$$M = \begin{bmatrix} 1 & x_1 & x_1^2 & \cdots & x_1^n \\ 1 & x_2 & x_2^2 & \cdots & x_2^n \\ & & \vdots & & \\ 1 & x_{n+1} & x_{n+1}^2 & \cdots & x_{n+1}^n \end{bmatrix}$$

$$\mathbf{a} = (a_0, a_1, \ldots, a_n) \quad \text{and} \quad \mathbf{y} = (y_1, y_2, \ldots, y_{n+1})$$

Hence, the coefficients of the polynomial $p(x)$ can be found by solving the matrix equation $M\mathbf{a} = \mathbf{y}$ for a. Note that $M = [x_i^{j-1}]$. Matrices of this form are called *Vandermonde matrices*. It is a theorem that Vandermonde matrices are invertible, so the equation $M\mathbf{a} = \mathbf{y}$ has a unique solution. In what follows, the polynomial

$$p(x) = a_0 + a_1 x + \cdots + a_4 x^4$$

passing through the points $(1, 5)$, $(2, 3)$, $(3, 27)$, $(4, 12)$, and $(5, 2)$ is derived. Such data points might represent instrument readings taken at 1:00, 2:00, 3:00, 4:00, and 5:00 o'clock.

| *You can use Maple's* **vandermonde** *command to generate the coefficient matrix M.* | ```
y:=vector([5,3,27,12,2]);
M:=vandermonde([1,2,3,4,5]);
```<br>Note the form of $M$. |
| *The vector of coefficients of p is the solution of the equation* **Mx = y.** | ```
a:=linsolve(M,y);
```<br>The components of $a$ are the coefficients of $p(x)$. |
| *You can now compute the polynomial p either as an expression or as a function.* | ```
p:=x->dotprod(
a,vector([seq(x^i,i=0..4)]));
```<br>You might wish to double check the value of $p(x)$ at $x = 1, 2, 3, 4, 5$. |
| *You can plot the graph of the polynomial p for more information.* | ```
plot(p,x=0..6);
```<br>As usual, you may have to experiment with the plot parameters to get the desired information. |

Summary and Extensions

Maple knows all the standard matrix and vector functions: **det**, **transpose**, **inverse**, and so on.

Every square matrix is a root of its own characteristic polynomial.

Vandermonde matrices arise naturally in curve fitting. It is a theorem that any Vandermonde matrix is invertible.

Maple's symbolic capabilities can be used to verify important theorems (with possibly obscure proofs) in low dimensions. In many cases, you can use the **seq** command to save typing.

Related Commands **companion**.

Additional Activities

1. Compute the angle between the vectors $\mathbf{u} = (1, 2, 3, 5)$ and $\mathbf{v} = (3, -2, 2/3, 4)$. Convert the angle to degrees and get a floating-point approximation.

2. Use the **vandermonde** and **linsolve** commands to find the polynomial $p = a_0 + a_1x + a_2x^2 + a_3x^3 + a_4x^4 + a_5x^5$

passing through the six points $(-6, 12)$, $(-3/2, -2)$, $(1/4, 3)$, $(3/4, 11)$, $(47, 33)$, and $(11, -27)$.

3. Let M be the matrix

$$\begin{bmatrix} 0 & 1 & 1 & 1 & 1 \\ 1 & 0 & 1 & 1 & 1 \\ 1 & 1 & 0 & 1 & 1 \\ 1 & 1 & 1 & 0 & 1 \\ 1 & 1 & 1 & 1 & 0 \end{bmatrix}$$

and let A be the submatrix obtained by deleting the fifth column of A. Compute the rank of A. Because the rank cannot exceed the number of columns, the matrix A is said to be of *full* rank. Show that the matrix $A^T A$ is invertible. It is a theorem that for any $m \times n$ matrix A of rank n, the matrix $A^T A$ is invertible. Can you see why?

4. It is a theorem that the matrix B obtained by interchanging the first and second rows of a square matrix A has determinant $-\det(A)$. Verify this for a symbolic 4×4 matrix A. *Note:* Because the determinant of a 4×4 matrix has 24 terms, you may prefer to verify that $\det(A) + \det(B) = 0$. (You may want to use the **swaprow** command.)

5. Let A be the matrix generated by the Maple command **A:= matrix(3,3,(i,j)->i+j-1 mod 3)**. Let

$$p(x) = x^{17} - 4x^{15} + 3/2x^6 - 1/2x^3 + 7x - 3$$

and let $r(x)$ be the remainder on dividing $p(x)$ by the characteristic polynomial of A. Show that $p(A) = r(A)$.

6. Apply the **factor** command to the determinant of the 4×4 matrix **V := vandermonde([a,b,c,d])**. This will reveal one of the reasons why the Vandermonde matrix is so well known.

7. Every monic polynomial is the characteristic polynomial of a suitably chosen matrix. One of the simplest matrices having characteristic polynomial p is called the *companion matrix* of p and denoted **companion(p,x)** in Maple.

   a. Verify that $p = x^{12} - 32x^{10} + 11x^4 - 32x + 17$ is the characteristic polynomial of its companion matrix.

   b. Find a formula for the companion matrix.

4.5   Maple's Basis and Dimension Commands

One of the most useful ways to describe a vector space is by specifying a basis; Maple has a number of built-in commands that can help you do this.

As always...

```
with(linalg);
```

If M is any matrix, the nonzero rows of the reduced row echelon form are a basis for the row space of M.

```
M:=matrix(9,7,(i,j)->i+j mod 2);
F:=rref(M);
B:={row(F,1),row(F,2)};
```
The set *B* of nonzero rows of *F* is a basis for the row space of *M*.

Maple's **rowspace** *command will compute this basis for you.*

```
rowspace(M);
```
Hence, the row space of *M* consists of all vectors of the form (x, y, x, y, x, y, x).

The **colspace** *command works analogously.*

```
colspace(M);
```
The **colspace** command applies **rowspace** to the transpose of the specified matrix. The vectors returned are a *basis* for the column space of *M*. Note that the column space consists of all vectors of the form (x, y, x, y, x).

You can also use Maple's **basis** *command to obtain a basis from any spanning set.*

```
for i to 9
  do
     u.i:=vector(7,j->i+j)
  od;
SpanList:=[seq(u.i,i=1..9)];
B:=basis(SpanList);
```
The argument to the **basis** command can be any set or list of vectors. The result is a subset or sublist of the vectors passed to **basis**.

If you require an orthogonal basis, you can apply Maple's **GramSchmidt** *command.*

```
GS:=GramSchmidt(B);
```
The argument to **GramSchmidt** can be either a set or a list of vectors. The result is an orthogonal set or list of vectors with the same span as the original. The vectors passed to **GramSchmidt** need not be linearly independent.

The (nonzero) vectors can be normalized by dividing each by its norm.

```
T:=[seq(GS[i]/norm(GS[i],2),i=1..2)];
```
The *i*th element of the list *GS* is *GS[i]*. Recall that the standard vector norm is denoted **norm(v,2)** in Maple.

The **colspace** *command returns a basis for the range of the matrix function* **x** → *M***x**.

```
colspace(M);
```
Is the result what you expected?

You can obtain the dimension of the row or column space without computing a basis.

```
rank(M);
```
You might wish to compare the rank of *M* to the rank of M^T. Your text says they should agree. You might also wish to compare the rank of *M* to the rank of the product $M^T M$. Can you think of any reason why they should agree?

You can use the **nullspace** *command to get a basis for the kernel of the command* **x** → *M***x**.

```
K:=nullspace(M);
```
The **nullspace** command is also called **kernel**.

You may wish to compare the output of **nullspace** *to that of* **linsolve**.

```
linsolve(M,vector(9,i->0));
```
The **linsolve** routine returns a general, parameterized solution, from which it is easy to derive a basis for the solution space; **nullspace** returns a basis directly.

Sums and Intersections of Subspaces

Assume U and V are subspaces of R^n spanned by $C = \{u_1, u_2, \ldots, u_r\}$ and $D = \{v_1, v_2, \ldots, v_s\}$, respectively.

```
C:={seq(vector(7,j->min(i,j)),i=1..5)};
D:={seq(vector(7,j->max(i,j)),i=1..4)};
```

In this particular case, both C and D are linearly independent sets.

```
basis(C);
basis(D);
```
Hence *U* and *V* have dimensions 5 and 4, respectively.

You can use Maple's **sumbasis** *command to find a basis for the subspace U + V.*

```
sumbasis(C,D);
```
The subspace *U* + *V* is spanned by *C* ∪ *D*. Notice that *U* + *V* has dimension 6.

You can also use Maple's **intbasis** *command to find a basis for the intersection U ∩ V.*

```
intbasis(C,D);
```
Note the relation between dim(*U* + *V*) and dim(*U*) + dim(*V*) − dim(*U* ∩ *V*). Can you prove this in general?

Summary and Extensions

Maple provides the commands **rowspace**, **colspace**, **kernel**, **nullspace**, and **basis** for finding bases of subspaces. You can use the **GramSchmidt** command to get an orthogonal basis for a subspace.

Related Commands **rowspan**, **colspan**.

Additional Activities

1. Find a basis B for the subspace U of R^5 spanned by the vectors $\mathbf{v}_1 = (1, 3, 5, 7, 9)$, $\mathbf{v}_2 = (3, 5, 7, 9, 11)$, $\mathbf{v}_3 = (5, 7, 9, 11, 13)$, $\mathbf{v}_4 = (7, 9, 11, 13, 15)$.

2. Let M be the augmented matrix $M = [\mathbf{v}_1, \mathbf{v}_2, \mathbf{v}_3, \mathbf{v}_4]$ with ith column vector $\mathbf{v}_i$ from Activity 1. Find bases for the null space and range of M, and find the rank of M.

3. Use **GramSchmidt** on the basis B of Activity 1 to find an orthogonal basis for U.

4. Use the result of Activity 3 to find an orthonormal basis T for the subspace U of Activity 1.

5. Use **randmatrix** with the **sparse** option to generate a 10×10 matrix M. Use Maple's **intbasis** command to verify that the row space of M has a trivial intersection with the null space of M.

6. Pick two subsets B and C of R^{10} at random. (You can use the **randmatrix** command and use the rows of the result.) Use Maple's **sumbasis**, **basis**, and **intbasis** commands to verify that the dimension of the span of $B \cup C$ is the dimension of the span of B plus the dimension of the span of C minus the dimension of the intersection of the span of B and the span of C.

4.6 Linear Transformations

You can define a linear transformation using either an arrow-style definition or a **proc** definition.

This defines a linear transformation from R^5 to R^3.

```
L:=x->vector([2*x[1]-x[2],
x[4]+3*x[5],3*x[5]+1/2*x[4]]);
```

Note that the Maple definition of *L* does not restrict its domain to R^5—or even to vectors for that matter.

As defined, L cannot successfully be applied to expressions—even if they evaluate to a vector in R^5.

```
u:=vector(5,i->i);
v:=vector(5,i->i!);
L(u+v);
```

You could use **L(evalm(u+v))** here.

*Using a **proc**-style definition, you can define linear transformations that will evaluate expressions. The linear transformation T, defined here, has this property.*

```
T:=
  proc(x)
    local y;
    y:=evalm(x);
    vector([2*y[1]+3*y[2],
    -3*y[1]+y[3],3*y[1]-2*y[3]]);
  end;
```

Notice that *T* applies **evalm** to its own argument. The second line of the definition confines the effect of assigning *y* to the internal workings of the procedure itself.

The linear transformation T can be applied to expressions involving both numerical and symbolic vectors.

```
u:=vector([5,-7,9]);
v:=vector(3);
T(u+k*v);
```

The standard matrix of a linear transformation can be easily determined by applying it to a symbolic vector.

```
T(v);
A:=matrix([
[2,3,0],
[-3,0,1],
[3,0,-2]]);
```

The (i, j)-entry of *A* is the coefficient of $v[j]$ in the *i*th component of $T(\mathbf{v})$.

*You can also use Maple's **genmatrix** command to compute A.*

```
genmatrix(
[T(v)[1],T(v)[2],T(v)[3]],
[v[1],v[2],v[3]]);
```

Note that the first argument is the list of components of $T(\mathbf{v})$ and the second argument is the list of components of **v**.

You can make the calcu-
lation of the matrix even
easier by converting the
vectors to lists.

```
TT:=convert(T(v),list);
vv:=convert(v,list);
genmatrix(TT,vv);
```
This is particularly helpful for larger matrices.

You can easily verify that
$T(\mathbf{v}) = A\mathbf{v}$ *in general.*

```
T(v);
evalm(A&*v);
```

You can find the kernel and
range of T from A.

```
kernel(A);
colspace(A);
```
If a linear transformation L is specified by a collection of equations $L(\mathbf{b}_i) = \mathbf{d}_i$, $i = 1 \ldots k$, where $\{\mathbf{b}_1, \mathbf{b}_2, \ldots, \mathbf{b}_k\}$ is a basis for V, you can easily create a Maple procedure that returns $L(\mathbf{v})$ for any vector $\mathbf{v}$ in V. Note that if $\mathbf{v} = a_1\mathbf{b}_1 + \cdots + a_5\mathbf{b}_5$, then $L(\mathbf{v}) = a_1\mathbf{d}_1 + \cdots + a_5\mathbf{d}_5$.

Here are two collections
$\mathbf{b}_1, \ldots, \mathbf{b}_5$ *and* $\mathbf{d}_1, \ldots, \mathbf{d}_5$ *of*
vectors in R^7. *The vectors*
$\mathbf{b}_1, \ldots, \mathbf{b}_5$ *are a basis for the*
subspace V they span.

```
for j to 5
  do
    b.j:=vector(7,i->min(i,j))
  od;
for j to 5
  do
    d.j:=vector(7,i->
      sum(r,r=max(j-i+1,0)..j))
  od;
```

If $\mathbf{v} = a_1\mathbf{b}_1 + \cdots + a_5\mathbf{b}_5$
is any vector in V, then the
coefficients $a_1, a_2, \ldots, a_5$
can be obtained by us-
ing **linsolve** *with*
the augmented matrix
$B = [\mathbf{b}_1, \ldots, \mathbf{b}_5]$.

```
B:=augment(seq(b.i,i=1..5));
v:=vector([1,7,9,4,2,2,2]);
a:=linsolve(B,v);
```
You may recall that if a vector $\mathbf{u}$ lies outside the span of $[\mathbf{b}_1, \ldots, \mathbf{b}_5]$, then **linsolve(B,u)** will give no response, not even an error message. The vector $\mathbf{a} = (a_1, a_2, \ldots, a_5)$ is called the coordinate vector of $\mathbf{v}$ with respect to the basis $B = \{\mathbf{b}_1, \ldots, \mathbf{b}_5\}$.

$L(\mathbf{v})$ *is now given by*
$a_1\mathbf{d}_1 + \cdots + a_5\mathbf{d}_5 = D\mathbf{a}$,
where D is the augmented
matrix $[\mathbf{d}_1, \ldots, \mathbf{d}_5]$.

```
D:=augment(seq(d.i,i=1..5));
w:=evalm(D&*a);
```
Notice that the result is assigned the name **w**.

These steps can easily be
combined into a procedure.

```
L:=x->evalm(D&*linsolve(B,x));
```
Note that L will apply to any vector the same steps that were applied to $\mathbf{v}$. You might wish to verify this by comparing $L(\mathbf{v})$ with $\mathbf{w}$.

Orthogonal Projection

If U is a subspace of R^n and $\mathbf{v} \in R^n$, then the element of U closest to $\mathbf{v}$ is the orthogonal projection of $\mathbf{v}$ onto U. The orthogonal projection of a vector $\mathbf{v}$ in R^n onto the column space of a matrix A is the vector $\mathbf{w}$ closest to $\mathbf{v}$ for which the equation $A\mathbf{x} = \mathbf{w}$ has solution. The vector $\mathbf{w}$ is unique and the map $\mathbf{v} \rightarrow \mathbf{w}$ is a linear transformation. The solution of the equation $A\mathbf{x} = \mathbf{w}$ is called the least squares (or "best approximate") solution of the equation $A\mathbf{x} = \mathbf{v}$. In Maple, the best approximate solution of the equation $A\mathbf{x} = \mathbf{v}$ is denoted **leastsqrs(A,v)**.

You can use Maple's **leastsqrs** *command to get an approximate solution of a vector equation* $A\mathbf{x} = \mathbf{v}$. *If an exact solution exists, it will be given.*

```
R:=randmatrix(5,4);
v:=vector([1,1,1,1,1]);
a:=leastsqrs(R,v);
```
The vector $\mathbf{a}$ is chosen so that the distance from $R\mathbf{a}$ to $\mathbf{v}$ is minimized.

You can use the result $\mathbf{a}$ *of* **leastsqrs(R,v)** *to compute the orthogonal projection of* $\mathbf{v}$ *onto the column space of R.*

```
w:=evalm(R&*a);
```
The vector $\mathbf{w}$ is the best approximation to $\mathbf{v}$ that lies in the column space of the matrix A. The vector $\mathbf{w}$ can also be obtained as the sum

$$(\mathbf{v} \cdot \mathbf{r}_1)\mathbf{r}_1 + (\mathbf{v} \cdot \mathbf{r}_2)\mathbf{r}_2 + \cdots + (\mathbf{v} \cdot \mathbf{r}_5)\mathbf{r}_5$$

where $\{\mathbf{r}_1, \mathbf{r}_2, \ldots, \mathbf{r}_5\}$ is an orthonormal basis for the column space of R.

Summary

You can easily write a Maple procedure to implement the definition of a linear transformation as a function.

Maple's symbolic capabilities allow you to find the standard matrix of a linear transformation from R^n to R^n.

You can automate the computation of the matrix of a linear transformation by using **genmatrix**.

You can convert vectors to lists (or sets) using Maple's **convert** command.

Use **leastsqrs** to get an approximate solution of an equation $A\mathbf{x} = \mathbf{b}$. The exact solution is returned if one exists.

You can use **leastsqrs** and matrix multiplication to compute the orthogonal projection of a vector onto the column space of a matrix.

Additional Activities

1. Let $A = [a_{ij}]$ be the 7×7 matrix defined by

$$a_{ij} = \begin{cases} 0 & \text{if } i = j \\ 1 & \text{if } i \neq j \end{cases}$$

   For each $i = 1 \ldots 7$, let $\mathbf{b}_i$ be the ith row vector of A and let $\mathbf{c}_i = (i, i + 1, i + 2, i + 3, i + 4, i + 5, i + 6)$. Assume that T is a linear transformation satisfying $T(\mathbf{b}_i) = \mathbf{c}_i$, for $i = 1 \ldots 7$. Find a formula for T and the standard matrix of T.

2. Find the kernel and range of the linear transformation T of Activity 1.

3. Given a basis $B = \{\mathbf{b}_1, \mathbf{b}_2, \ldots, \mathbf{b}_k\}$ for a vector space V, any vector $\mathbf{v}$ in V has unique expression

$$\mathbf{v} = a_1\mathbf{b}_1 + a_2\mathbf{b}_2 + \cdots + a_k\mathbf{b}_k$$

   The k-tuple $(a_1, a_2, \ldots, a_k)$ is called the B-coordinate vector of $\mathbf{v}$. The map that takes each vector $\mathbf{v}$ to its B-coordinate vector is a linear transformation. Let $B = \{\mathbf{b}_1, \ldots, \mathbf{b}_6\}$ be the basis for R^6 defined by $\mathbf{b}_i[j] = \min(i, j)$. Define a procedure **Coord** that takes every vector $\mathbf{v}$ in R^6 to its B-coordinate vector.

4. Find the standard matrix of the linear transformation **Coord** of Activity 3.

5. If B and D are two bases for a vector space V, then the map that takes the B-coordinate vector of every vector $\mathbf{v}$ to the D-coordinate vector of $\mathbf{v}$ is a linear transformation. Let B be as in Activity 3, and let D be the basis for R^6 defined by $d_j[i] :=$ sum$(r, r = \max(j - i + 1, 0, \ldots, j))$. Define a function L that takes the B-coordinate vector of any $\mathbf{v}$ in R^6 to the D-coordinate vector of $\mathbf{v}$.

6. Find the standard matrix of the linear transformation L of Activity 5.

7. Find the "best approximate solution" to the equation $M\mathbf{x} = \mathbf{v}$, where $\mathbf{v} = (1, 2, 3, 4, 5)$ and $M = [m_{ij}]$ is the 5×3 matrix with $m_{ij} = 1$, for all i, j.

8. In Activity 7, find the orthogonal projection of the vector $\mathbf{v} = (1, 2, 3, 4, 5)$ onto the column space of the matrix M.

4.7   Eigenvalues and Eigenvectors

Eigenvalues and eigenvectors, also known as characteristic values and characteristic vectors, are among the most frequently applied topics commonly studied in undergraduate mathematics. For example, if multiplication by A represents the action of the forces on a physical system with components represented by the vector $\mathbf{v}$, and if $A\mathbf{v} = \lambda\mathbf{v}$, then the components of the system are all changing at the same rate. If $\lambda = 1$, then the system is static.

In this section, all matrices have rational entries. This implies that the characteristic polynomials of the matrices considered will have rational coefficients, but it does not imply that the eigenvalues are rational. Maple is capable of describing the eigenvalues and eigenvectors of any rational matrix—within the limits imposed by the time and resources available to it.

If you are beginning a new session:

```
with(linalg);
alias(ID=&*());
```

Here is a 4 × 4 matrix that is fairly typical of those commonly used to study eigenvalue/eigenvector problems.

```
f:=
  proc(i,j)
    if i<3 and j<3
      then min(i,j)
    elif j>= 3
      then max(i,j)
    else 0
    fi
  end;
A:=matrix(4,4,f);
```

Compute the characteristic polynomial of A.

```
det(x - A);
```
Maple treats the unassigned variable x as a scalar.

Maple also has built-in commands for computing the characteristic matrix and characteristic polynomial.	```charmat(A,x);```
	```p:=charpoly(A,x);```
	Note that a second argument has to be specified in each case. The second argument can be either an undefined variable, as it is here, or a constant.

You can use the **solve** *command to find the eigenvalues.*	```solve(p=0,x);``` The eigenvalues are the terms of the sequence returned.

Alternately, you can use the built-in **eigenvals** *command to perform the same operations.*	```eigenvals(A);```
	```lambda:={"};```
	Note that there are three distinct eigenvalues λ_1, λ_2, and λ_3, two of multiplicity 1 and one of multiplicity 2; placing them in a set removes the duplication.

For each i, the λ_i-eigenspace is the solution space of the matrix $(\lambda_i I - A)\mathbf{x} = 0$.	```Z:=vector(4,i->0);```
	```linsolve(lambda[1]-A,Z);```
	This is a parametric description of the vectors in the λ_1-eigenspace.

You can also use the built-in **nullspace** *command to get a basis for the eigenspaces.*	```nullspace(lambda[1]-A);``` The set returned is a basis for the λ_1-eigenspace. You may wish to repeat the process for the other two eigenvalues.
One special property of the matrix A is that its characteristic polynomial has no factors of degree greater than 2.	```factor(p);``` The factor command returns a factorization of the form $rp_1^{e_1}p_2^{e_2}\ldots p_k^{e_k}$, where r is a rational number and each p_i is a nonconstant polynomial with integer coefficients. The approach used for A will work for any (rational) matrix, as long as none of the factors p_i of the characteristic polynomial has degree 3 or greater.

In general, however, characteristic polynomials can have factors of any degree.	```B:=matrix(5,5,f);```
	```p:=det(x-B);```
	```factor(p);```
	The characteristic polynomial has two factors, one of degree 3 and one of degree 2.

In this case, the descriptions of the eigenvalues are much more complicated.	```eigenvals(B);``` The complexity of the description by radicals of a root of a factor of degree 3 or higher is a barrier that complicates the computation of the eigenvectors of matrices larger than 2 × 2. To break through this barrier, Maple provides a simpler representation of the roots of the characteristic polynomial that will function with **nullspace**

and **linsolve**: If p is a polynomial in x, then **RootOf(p,x)** is a parameter that can stand for any of the roots of the polynomial p.

The **RootOf** *command is typically applied to the factors of the characteristic polynomial. Note that a factor of degree n has exactly n (distinct, but possibly complex) roots.*

```
facts:=factor(charpoly(B,x));
p1:=op(facts)[1];
lambda[1]:=RootOf(p1,x);
```
The **op** command returns the sequence of factors. In this case, $r = 1$ in the factorization $rp_1^{e_1} p_2^{e_2} \ldots p_k^{e_k}$ of the characteristic polynomial, so Maple simplifies the factorization to $p_1^{e_1} p_2^{e_2} \ldots p_k^{e_k}$. Hence, **op(facts)[1]** is p_1. Each root of each p_i has multiplicity e_i as a root of p.

Either **nullspace** *or* **linsolve** *can now be used to obtain a description of the eigenvectors.*

```
nullspace(lambda[1]-B);
```
It is important to keep in mind that the (apparently) single basis returned actually represents more than one basis, one for each of the roots of p_1.

You can simplify the notation considerably by aliasing an unassigned variable to the **RootOf**.

```
alias(t=lambda[1]);
NS:=nullspace(t-B);
```
Notice that the result has been assigned the name *NS*.

You can use Maple's **all-values** *command to convert a* **RootOf** *into radical form whenever this is possible.*

```
all:=allvalues(t);
```
The translation to radical form can be made as long as the parameter is a **RootOf** of a polynomial of degree 4 or less. There is no description by radicals, in general, of the roots of a polynomial of degree 5 or greater. When **allvalues** cannot find a description by radicals, it will attempt to find decimal approximations of the exact answers.

If you wish, you can substitute the radical forms for t in the basis vector(s).

```
ES[1]:=subs(t=all[1],NS);
```
Similar statements substituting give the bases for the eigenspaces associated with the other root(s) of p_1.

A few properties of **RootOf** *worth noting:*

```
RootOf(3,x);
RootOf(2*x-3/2,x);
RootOf((x^2-1)^2,x);
```
In the first case, there are no roots. In the second case, the root is computed and returned. In the third case, some simplification is performed.

If you want all of the irrational eigenvalues of a matrix in **RootOf** *form, you can use the* **eigenvals** *command with the* **implicit** *option.*

```
eigenvals(A,implicit);
```
You use the **implicit** option by using **implicit** as a second argument to **eigenvals**.

Once you are familiar with the use of **RootOf**, you can interpret the result returned by Maple's **eigenvects** command.

You can use **eigenvects** *to get both the eigenvalues and eigenvectors.*

```
C:=matrix(6,6,f);
eigenvects(C);
```
Note that the result is a sequence of lists. Each list is of the form

$$[\lambda, n, \{\mathbf{v}_1, \mathbf{v}_2, \ldots, \mathbf{v}_s\}]$$

where λ is an eigenvalue (either a rational number or a **RootOf**), n is the multiplicity of λ as a root of the characteristic polynomial, and the set $\{\mathbf{v}_1, \mathbf{v}_2, \ldots, \mathbf{v}_s\}$ is a basis for the λ-eigenspace.

It is frequently important to know whether the eigenvalues of a matrix are rational, real, or complex. If the eigenvalues are in radical form, Maple's complex number evaluator, **evalc**, will attempt to write them in the form $a + bi$, with a and b real.

Use **evalc** *to see if the eigenvalues are real.*

```
allc:=evalc([all]);
simplify(");
```
If applied to a list or set, **evalc** is automatically mapped onto the entries of the list or set. This is true for lists as well, but not for sequences or arrays.

Recall that **all** was assigned the value returned by **all-values(t)** above. The complex terms are gone; all the eigenvalues are real.

If you want more information on the eigenvalues, you can also apply the **evalf** command. However, there is always some possibility that rounding errors may mislead you.

Use **evalf** *for a floating-point evaluation.*

```
evalf(");
```
If applied to a set, **evalf**, like **evalc**, is automatically mapped onto the elements of the set.

You might like to try using the **evalf** and **evalc** commands in the other order to see a small effect of rounding errors. For factors of degree 5 or greater, floating-point approximation and graphing are the only tools available other than **RootOf**. Techniques for exploring roots of polynomials with Maple were discussed at some length in Chapter 2.

You unalias a variable by aliasing it to itself.

```
alias(t=t);
```

Notice that whenever the **alias** command is used, it lists all aliased variables.

Summary

You can use either the **factor** command or the **eigenvals** command to investigate the eigenvalues of a matrix. The **RootOf** command makes it possible to describe the eigenvalues and eigenvectors of any rational matrix. Use either **linsolve** or **null-space** to find the eigenvectors associated with a particular eigenvalue. Use the **allvalues** command to convert **RootOf** to radical expressions, if possible. If exact radical answers are not possible, floating-point approximations will be returned. You can use **evalc** and **simplify** to determine whether eigenvalues are real or complex. You can also use **evalf** for the same purpose, though it is often better to use **evalc** first.

Additional Activities

1. Find all the eigenvalues and eigenvectors of the 9×9 matrix $A = [a_{ij}]$ with $a_{ij} = 1$ for all i and j.

2. Find all the eigenvalues and eigenvectors of the companion matrix of the polynomial

$$p = 1 - x + x^2 - x^3 + x^4$$

Determine which of the eigenvalues are rational, which are real, and which are complex.

3. Find the eigenvalues and eigenvectors of the 4×4 matrix $B = [b_{ij}]$, where, for each i and j, b_{ij} is the smaller of i and j. Determine which of the eigenvalues are rational, which are real, and which are complex.

4. Find the eigenvalues and eigenvectors of the 3×3 matrix $Q = [q_{ij}]$, where, for each i and j, $q_{ij} = i/j$. Determine which of the eigenvalues are rational, which are real, and which are complex.

4.8   Diagonalization and Similarity

Two problems are associated with diagonalization. The first is to determine whether a given matrix A is diagonalizable (that is, similar to a diagonal matrix). If this is the case, then you may also want to find a diagonalizing matrix P (that is, an invertible matrix P satisfying $P^{-1}AP = D$, where D is a diagonal matrix). Recall that an $n \times n$ matrix A is diagonalizable if and only if it has n linearly independent eigenvectors. This, in turn, is equivalent to the condition that for each eigenvalue λ of A, the dimension of the λ-eigenspace is equal to the multiplicity of λ as a root of the characteristic polynomial. The restriction to rational matrices continues.

Diagonalization

If you have not already done so:

```
with(linalg);
alias(ID=&*());
```

The matrix A is a good, simple first example.

```
f:=
   proc(i,j)
      if i=j
         then 0
         else 1
         fi
      end;
A:=matrix(9,9,f);
```

The matrix A is symmetric and therefore diagonalizable. The diagonalizability is also obvious from the information returned by **eigenvects**.

```
eigsys:=eigenvects(A);
```
The basis for the *i*th eigenspace is the third component of **eigsys[i]**. Notice that for each eigenvalue λ, the dimension of the λ-eigenspace is the same as the multiplicity of λ as a root of the characteristic polynomial.

The basis vectors of the eigenspaces are used to form a diagonalizing matrix.

```
ES[1]:=eigsys[1][3];
ES[2]:=eigsys[2][3];
```

You can use **op** *and* **augment** *to construct the diagonalizing matrix.*

```
P:=augment(op(ES[1]),op(ES[2]));
```
The **op** command returns the contents of the sets as sequences. Two sequences separated by a comma form a sequence, so this command applies **augment** to the sequence of eigenvectors in the bases.

Because there are no horrendously complicated expressions in either A or P, Maple can verify that $P^{-1}AP$ is diagonal.

```
evalm(inverse(P)&*A&*P);
```
The eigenvalues appear on the diagonal according to the ordering of the vectors in *P*. You might wish to compare this result with that obtained if the roles of *ES*[1] and *ES*[2] are reversed in the definition of *P*.

The matrix B defined here presents an obstacle not encountered in diagonalizing A.

```
g:=
  proc(i,j)
    if i=1 and j=1
      then -1
    elif i<2
      then 0
    else max(i,j)
    fi
  end;
B:=matrix(5,5,g);
```

As a rule, you will probably want to apply **eigenvects**.

```
eigsys:=eigenvects(B);
```
It is clear that there are no complex components in any of the eigenspace basis vectors associated with the eigenvalue -1. The situation regarding the other eigenvectors is somewhat less clear.

To simplify the descriptions returned by **eigenvects**, *it is helpful to give an* **alias** *to any* **RootOf** *that appears in an eigenvector.*

```
alias(t=RootOf(x^4-14*x^3-45*x^2-29*x-5,x));
eigsys;
```
If your system returns a different **RootOf**, use it instead of this one. Depending on your system, you may be able to copy the **RootOf** expression from the result of the **eigenvects** command and paste it into the **alias** command.

The computation of the other eigenspaces varies somewhat from the computations of the eigenspaces of A for $\lambda = -1$.

```
ES[1]:=eigsys[1][3];
```
One of the eigenvalues is in **RootOf** form—in our case, the second one. If the order of the results returned by **eigenvects** is different in your case, you will need to adjust the subscripts accordingly.

It is likely you will want to convert the **RootOf**s *to radical form for describing the diagonalizing matrix.*

```
all:=allvalues(t);
```
The conversion is not possible in all cases, but it is possible—and probably desirable—in this case.

You can obtain the other two eigenspace bases by simply using **subs**.

```
ES[2]:=subs(t=all[1],eigsys[2][3]);
ES[3]:=subs(t=all[2],eigsys[2][3]);
ES[4]:=subs(t=all[3],eigsys[2][3]);
ES[5]:=subs(t=all[4],eigsys[2][3]);
```

You can now build the diagonalizing matrix in the same manner you used for A.

```
Q:=augment(op(ES[1]),op(ES[2]),
op(ES[3]),op(ES[4]),op(ES[5]);
```

*For matrices with several eigenspaces, you may want to use the **seq** command to save some typing.*

```
Q:=augment(seq(op(ES[i]),i=1..5));
```

The definition of "several" is personal; this is shorter than the style used to define Q. The matrix Q diagonalizes B. But the time required for your computer to complete the calculation $Q^{-1}BQ$ will probably exceed your interest. This is due to the complexity of the descriptions of the entries.

Similarity and Smith Form

Two (square) matrices A and B are *similar* if B is of the form $P^{-1}AP$, and—surprisingly—this is the case if and only if their characteristic matrices $xI - A$ and $xI - B$ are *equivalent* (that is, if and only if $xI - B$ can be obtained from $xI - A$ by a sequence of elementary row and column operations). Every matrix M with polynomial entries can be transformed into an equivalent diagonal matrix $S = \text{diag}(1, \ldots, 1, p_1, p_2, \ldots, p_k, 0, \ldots, 0)$, where, for each i, p_i is a nonconstant factor of p_{i+1}. The matrix S is uniquely determined by M and is called the *Smith form* of M. Two matrices are equivalent if and only if they have the same Smith form. Hence, two numerical matrices A and B are similar if and only if their characteristic matrices $xI - A$ and $xI - B$ have the same Smith form. (The elementary operations **mulrow** and **mulcol** are restricted to multiplication by scalars to make the operations reversible. Notice that this restriction is not necessary for **addrow** and **addcol**.)

Maple can compute the Smith form of any matrix with polynomial entries.

```
M:=matrix(3,3,(i,j)->x^i-j);
smith(M,x);
```

Smith form can be used to determine whether two matrices are similar. (Although the current assumption is that all matrices have rational entries, the theory is not restricted to this case.)

```
d:=
  proc(i,j)
    if i<j
      then 0
    else 1
    fi
  end;
```

```
G:=matrix(4,4,d);
H:=transpose(G);
smith(charmat(G,x),x);
smith(charmat(H,x),x);
```
In this case, the Smith forms of the characteristic matrices are the same, so the matrices are similar. (Actually, every matrix is similar to its transpose.)

Similarity and Frobenius Form

It follows from the previous section on Smith form that the polynomials on the diagonal of the Smith form of the matrix $xI - A$ determine completely the matrices similar to A. Not surprisingly, the companion matrices of these polynomials also determine the similarity class of A. The block diagonal matrix F (with blocks that are the companion matrices of these nonconstant polynomials) is called the *Frobenius form* of A. The Frobenius form has two clear advantages. One is that the Frobenius form of a rational matrix is rational. Another is that a matrix is similar to its Frobenius form. You can obtain the Frobenius form (sometimes called the "rational canonical" form, though this term is not used uniformly) with the **frobenius** command.

If you have not already done so:
```
with(linalg);
alias(ID=&*());
```

Consider the matrix G defined here.
```
d:=
   proc(i,j)
     if i<j
       then 0
     else 1
       fi
     end;
G:=matrix(4,4,d);
```
G is the same matrix used in the previous section.

Compute the Frobenius form of G.
```
FG:=frobenius(G);
```
In this case, the Frobenius form is the companion matrix of the characteristic polynomial.

Compare the Smith forms of   `smith(x-G,x);`
xI − G and xI − FG.   `smith(x-FG,x);`
Note that they are the same, although you may have to expand the (4, 4)-entry of the first matrix to see this. It follows that G is similar to FG.

Summary

Using **eigenvects**, it is easy to determine whether a (rational) matrix is diagonalizable. If a matrix A is diagonalizable, you can build a diagonalizing matrix P from the eigenspace bases returned by **eigenvects** by using **op** and **augment**. You can determine whether two matrices A and B are similar by comparing the Smith forms of their characteristic matrices. You can determine whether two matrices A and B are similar by comparing their Frobenius forms.

Additional Activities

1. Let $A = [a_{ij}]$ be the 5×5 matrix with

$$a_{ij} = \begin{cases} i + j - 1 & \text{if } i = j \\ i + j + 1 & \text{if } i \neq j \end{cases}$$

Determine whether A is diagonalizable and, if so, find a diagonalizing matrix P.

2. Let $\mathbf{B} = [\mathbf{b}_{ij}]$ be the 5×5 matrix with

$$b_{ij} = \begin{cases} 2 & \text{if } i = j \\ 1 & \text{if } i \neq j \end{cases}$$

Determine whether A is diagonalizable and, if so, find a diagonalizing matrix P.

3. Let $H = [h_{ij}]$ be the 4×4 matrix defined by $h_{ij} = 1/(i + j - 1)$. Determine whether H is diagonalizable and, if so, find a diagonalizing matrix. (H is the 4×4 *Hilbert matrix*.)

4. Let $p = 1 - x + x^2 - x^3 + x^4$ and $q = 1 - x + x^2$ have companion matrices A_{11} and A_{22}, respectively. Let A be the

6×6 matrix described in block form as

$$A = \begin{bmatrix} A_{11} & 0 \\ 0 & A_{22} \end{bmatrix}$$

Let C be the companion matrix of pq. Use the Smith forms of the characteristic matrices of A and C to show that A and C are similar.

5. Use the Frobenius forms of the matrices A and C of Activity 4 to show they are similar.

6. For three randomly generated 4×4 matrices A, show that A and its Frobenius form F are similar by verifying that $xI - A$ and $xI - F$ have the same Smith form.

Differential Equations

This chapter exploits Maple's powerful graphical, numerical, and symbolic capabilities to aid in understanding the often complex nature of differential equations.

5.1 Introduction

Maple requires some setup to take advantage of the routines described in this chapter.

A file called **ODE2** contains a number of routines you will use to analyze differential equations. The **ODE2** file is not part of Maple and must be read into each session for which it is used. This is similar to **with(student)**, which you used in the calculus section. However, the **ODE2** file is not built into Maple's library, although an older version is built into Maple's share library. Copy the file into the directory or folder that contains Maple or into your personal directory. Then type the following command:

*Reading the **ODE2** file into a Maple session.*

```
read ODE2;
```

This command is assumed for the rest of the chapter. Maple's capabilities, along with the procedures contained in the **ODE2** file, can be used to enhance understanding of the structure of differential equations. Maple can find explicit solutions to many differential equations. In cases where no closed-form solution exists, a wide variety of numerical schemes can be used to approximate solutions and get graphical information.

First-Order Differential Equations

First consider differential equations that can be written in the following form:

$$\frac{dy}{dt} = f(t, y) \tag{5.1}$$

A solution is a continuous function of t, which, when substituted for y, satisfies equation (5.1). You first need to translate the differential equation into a format Maple can recognize. Maple uses **diff(y(t),t)** to represent the derivative of y with respect to t. Consider solving the differential equation

$$\frac{dy}{dt} = t + y$$

Enter the differential equation.

```
deq1 := diff(y(t), t) = t + y(t);
```

The Maple command to solve differential equations is **dsolve**.

*Use **dsolve** to solve $dy/dt = t + y$.*

```
deq1sol := dsolve(deq1, y(t));
```
This produces the following output:

$$deq1sol := y(t) = -t - 1 + e^t\_C1$$

The **y(t)** in the **dsolve** command indicates that the differential equation is to be solved for $y(t)$. Maple returns the solution with an arbitrary constant, denoted **_C1**.

Whenever it finds an explicit solution, Maple returns an equation with $y(t)$ as the left-hand side and an expression on the right-hand side that gives the solution. This expression is useful for finding values of the solution or for generating plots. It is accessed using the **rhs** Maple command.

*Use **rhs** to access the expression defining the solution.*

```
rh1 := rhs(deq1sol);
```
The expression defining the solution is displayed. You can substitute a value for **_C1** into the right-hand side of the solution using the **subs** command and plot the resulting solution for several values of **_C1**.

You can plot several solutions for specific values of the constant.

```
plot(subs(_C1=1,rh1), subs(_C1=2,rh1),
     subs(_C1=0,rh1), subs(_C1=-1,rh1),
     subs(_C1=-2,rh1), t=-5..5, y=-5..5);
```

The graphs of these solutions over the range $-5 < t < 5$ and $-5 < y < 5$ are shown here. On your screen, each of the five solutions displays in a different color.

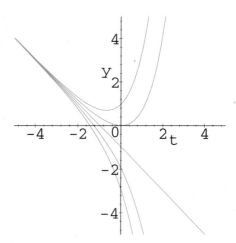

Several solutions to
$dy/dt = t + y.$

Maple will also solve a wide class of initial value problems. These are differential equations with an initial value such as $dy/dt = f(t, y)$, $y(t_0) = y_0$.

Solve the initial value problem, $\dfrac{dy}{dt} = \dfrac{1 - y - \sin(t)}{\cos(t)}$, $y(0) = 0.$

```
deq2  := diff(y(t), t) = (1 - y(t) -
    sin(t))/cos(t);
deq2init := y(0) = 0;
deq2sol := dsolve({deq2, deq2init}, y(t));
```

Note that the curly braces { and } are used to denote a set of objects in Maple—in this case, a set of equations. As a matter of consistency, you will always name the equations and the solutions. This is a good habit to develop.

You can plot this solution.

```
plot(rhs(deq2sol), t = -4..4, y = -3..3);
```

Note that the solution is not valid for all t and that, strictly speaking, the solution for which $y(0) = 0$ is defined only for the interval $-\pi/2 < t < 3\pi/2$. Maple also displays what looks like an asymptote, but this is really an artifact of using a computer. Maple connects the part of the solution that goes off the top of the plot with the part of the solution going off the bottom of the plot.

In some cases, the command **dsolve** will return an implicit solution—that is, a relationship between $y(t)$ and t. For example, when solving the equation $dy/dt = -t/y$, Maple gives an implicit solution.

Solve the equation $dy/dt = -t/y.$

```
deq3:= diff(y(t), t) = -t/y(t);
deq3sol:= dsolve(deq3, y(t));
```

This produces the following output:

$$deq3sol := y(t)^2 = -t^2 + \_C1$$

In some cases where Maple returns an implicit solution, Maple can find an explicit solution using an optional command called **explicit** in the **dsolve** command.

*Use **dsolve** with the explicit option to force Maple to find an explicit solution.*

```
deq3sol2 := dsolve(deq3, y(t), explicit);
```

Two solutions are returned in this case; these can be accessed as **deq3sol2[1]** and **deq3sol2[2]**. In situations where Maple returns more than one solution for an initial value problem, one has to be careful to check if both solutions work.

Using **fsolve** in an Application

*A physical example motivates the use of Maple's **subs** and **fsolve** commands.*

We will end this section by considering a physical example. Suppose a ball is thrown into the air with an initial velocity of 9.8 meters/second. How high does it go, and when does it hit the ground?

The motion of the ball is governed by Newton's second law of motion, which, in this case, gives the well-known equation $dv/dt = -g$, where g is the gravitational constant $g = 9.8$ meters/second^2 and v is the velocity.

The position of the ball is measured by its height in meters above the ground. Integrating twice, using the initial value for the velocity of 9.8 meters/second, and taking the initial position y to be zero, you obtain the following equations for the velocity $v(t)$ and the position $y(t)$:

$$v(t) = -9.8t + 9.8$$
$$y(t) = -4.9t^2 + 9.8t$$

To find how high the ball goes, solve for t in the equation $v(t) = 0$ and substitute this value into the equation for $y(t)$. You can verify that $v(1) = 0$ and $y(1) = 4.9$. The ball will hit the ground when $y(t) = 0$, which corresponds to $t = 2$. Using this value for t gives the velocity when the ball hits the ground: $v(2) = -9.8$ meters/second.

Taking air resistance into account provides a better model.

A more realistic model would be to include the force of air resistance. Assuming that the force due to air resistance is proportional to the velocity, Newton's second law of motion leads to the equation

$$\frac{dv}{dt} = -g - \frac{r}{m}v$$

In this equation m is the mass, taken to be 5 grams; g is the gravitational constant 9.8 meters/second^2; r is the coefficient of resistance, taken to be 2 grams/second; y is the position; and v is the velocity. You can use Maple to solve this equation for the velocity.

Input and solve the differential equation.

```
bveq := diff(v(t), t) = -g - r/m*v(t);
bvinit := v(0) = v0;
bvsol := dsolve({bveq, bvinit}, v(t));
```
The solution is returned explicitly. The velocity of the ball is given by

$$v(t) = - \left(gm - e^{-rt/m}(gm + v0\,r) \right) r^{-1}$$

The position $y(t)$ can be found by solving the differential equation $dy/dt = v(t)$. The expression **rhs(bvsol)** is the Maple expression for $v(t)$.

*Use **dsolve** to find the position function.*

```
bpeq := diff(y(t), t) = rhs(bvsol);
bpinit := y(0) = y0;
bpsol := dsolve({bpeq, bpinit}, y(t));
```
Again, an explicit solution is returned. A qualitative view of what air resistance does to the flight of the ball is given by the graph of position versus time for the equation with and without air resistance. In order to plot the solution, you need to substitute values for the constants g, m, r, $v0$, and $y0$.

Plot the position function with and without air resistance.

```
bcons := g = 9.8, m = 5, r = 2,
   v0 = 9.8, y0 = 0;
plot({subs(bcons, rhs(bpsol)),
   -4.9*t^2 + 9.8*t}, t = 0..2, 0..5.5);
```

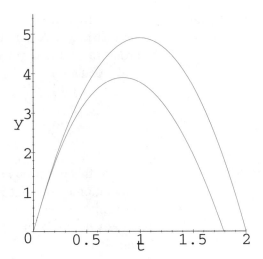

Position function for the ball with and without air resistance.

Use Maple's **fsolve** command to find the time when the velocity is zero. You find the maximum height by plugging the result of **fsolve** into the expression for the position.

Time and height of the ball when velocity is zero.

```
t1 := fsolve(subs({bcons, v(t) = 0},
   bvsol), t);
maxh := evalf(subs({t = t1, bcons}, bpsol));
```

The height when the velocity is zero is displayed. Similarly, to find the velocity when the ball hits the ground you use Maple's **fsolve** command to find the time when the position is zero. You then substitute this value into the expression for the velocity. Note that an optional third argument to **fsolve** is a range within which to look for the solution. This avoids the problem of finding other solutions that are not of interest in the problem.

Time and velocity when position is zero.

```
t2 := fsolve(subs({bcons, y(t) = 0},
   bpsol), t, 1.5 .. 2);
evalf(subs({bcons, t = t2}, bvsol));
```

The velocity at this other time is displayed.

Verifying Solutions

You can use Maple to verify your solutions.

At this point in your course in differential equations, you will have heard the phrase, "You *must* verify your solution by plugging it back into the differential equation," a few dozen times. Using **diff**, you can differentiate expressions and, using **subs**, you can have Maple verify your solutions.

A solution that is difficult to verify by paper-and-pencil methods.

Verify that $y(t) = -e^t + (e^{2t} + 2Ce^{-t})^{1/2}$ is a solution to the differential equation

$$\frac{y^2}{2} + 2ye^t + (y + e^t)\frac{dy}{dt} = 0$$

Input the information to verify the solution.

```
eq := y(t)^2/2 + 2*y(t)*exp(t)+
   (y(t) + exp(t))*diff(y(t), t) = 0;
sol:=-exp(t) + (exp(2*t)+
   2*C*exp(-t))^(1/2);
subs(y(t) = sol, eq);
simplify(");
```

Maple displays $0 = 0$, indicating that the expression substituted for $y(t)$ in the differential equation is indeed a solution. Notice the use of **%1** in the substituted equation and its subsequent definition immediately below.

Double checking the computer is just as important or more important than double checking your own work.

Computer algebra systems such as Maple are becoming more and more reliable. It is still fairly easy, however, to ask for something that makes no sense and get back answers. Consider the following:

```
dsolve({diff(y(t),t) = -t/y(t),
           y(0) = y0}, y(t));
```

which returns the following:

$$y(t) = -\sqrt{-t^2 + y0^2}, \ y(t) = \sqrt{-t^2 + y0^2}$$

Two solutions! Both cannot be right. The dilemma is that the solution depends on the sign of **y0**. Some experts would argue that Maple should not return a solution in this case or should return an error message. Most would agree, however, that the usability of the system is greatly enhanced and that more information can be gleaned from returning the two possible solutions. It is then up to the user to determine and verify which course of action to take next. You must be aware though that the system is not perfect and that you are most likely not a perfect user. You must use all available means to verify that what you are doing with the system is correct.

Additional Activities

1. Use **dsolve** to find the general solution for each of the initial value problems a–e. Plot the solution for several values of **C**.

a. $dy/dt = y$

b. $dy/dt = \frac{1}{2}y + t$

c. $dy/dt = t - y$

d. $dy/dt = 5y - 6e^{-t}$

e. $dy/dt = y^2$

2. A ball is thrown into the air with an initial velocity of 10 meters/second. Assuming air resistance proportional to velocity squared with constant of proportionality 0.2, find the maximum height of the ball. As long as the velocity is positive, the equation will be

$$\frac{dv}{dt} = -g - \frac{r}{m}v^2$$

   assuming that upward is the positive direction.

3. Continue Activity 2 for negative velocity. Here, the equation will be

$$\frac{dv}{dt} = -g + \frac{r}{m}v^2.$$

   Use your results from Activity 2 for the initial conditions in this equation and find the time and the velocity when the ball hits the ground.

4. Plot the expression for velocity in Activity 3 for the range $t = 0..20$. The velocity appears to reach a constant value. Find this value.

5.2 Numerically Graphing Solutions

You can use Maple to solve differential equations when no closed-form solution exists.

In this section you will consider ordinary differential equations in the form:

$$\frac{dx_1}{dt} = f_1(t, x_1, x_2, ..., x_n)$$

$$\frac{dx_2}{dt} = f_2(t, x_1, x_2, ..., x_n)$$

$$\vdots \qquad \vdots \qquad \vdots$$

$$\frac{dx_n}{dt} = f_n(t, x_1, x_2, ..., x_n)$$

Given an initial condition,

$$x_1(t_0) = x_1^0, x_2(t_0) = x_2^0, \ldots, x_n(t_0) = x_n^0$$

you can expect a solution defined near t_0 satisfying the equation and initial condition under certain assumptions. Essentially, the f_i and their partial derivatives should be continuous near t_0, although this is not always necessary.

Generally, you will not be able to write down closed-form solutions even with Maple's help. However, the computer is very good at approximating the solutions. We will discuss in detail later some of the algorithms used to numerically approximate solutions to differential equations. Remember that even familiar functions such as $\sin(t)$ and e^t are only approximated when you graph their solutions via computer.

The Maple procedure to plot solutions to differential equations is **orbitplot**.

There is a huge volume of mathematical literature devoted to numerically solving differential equations. Many of these algorithms are available in Maple. You will use the function **orbitplot**, which is part of the **ODE2** file, to graph numerical solutions. The basic usage is as follows:

The basic form of **orbitplot** procedure is

```
orbitplot(eq, <options>);
```

where **eq** is a differential equation that can be entered in a form similar to that in which you entered differential equations for **dsolve**. There are a myriad of options to control the appearance and method used to solve the differential equation. Two options that should always appear are the range over which the differential equation is to be integrated and at least one initial value.

Graph the solution to
$x' = y$
$y = -x$

```
orbitplot([diff(x(t), t) = y(t),
    diff(y(t), t) = -sin(x(t)) - 0.5*y(t)],
    t = 0..10, init = [0,0,3]);
```

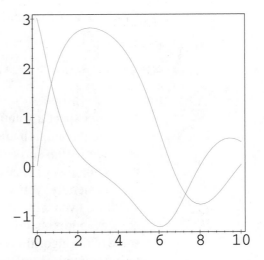

Solutions of
x′ = y
y′ = − sin(x) − y/2.

The default is to graph each dependent variable versus the independent variable. This can be changed with the **view** option, as we will see later. The default method for numerically integrating the differential equation is a simple fixed-step, fourth-order Runge/Kutta algorithm. The scheme is simple and fast, but solutions often appear jagged. Decreasing the step size with the **stepsize** option or, alternatively, increasing the number of steps taken over the *t*-range with the **numsteps** option will smooth out the graph and give a more accurate solution. Use the Help feature for details on all the options.

For many examples, a fixed-step algorithm will perform poorly or fail completely. A number of sophisticated variable step methods are available as options to **orbitplot**. The option **intmethod = besirk** is one method that works well on a variety of equations. This method is the result of Hendrick Kooijman and Ross Taylor, and the Maple implementation is the result of Kooijman, Taylor, and Schwalbe.[1]

The following example is known as van der Pol's equation and is used to model the heartbeat. Use some options to view the orbit in three dimensions along with the projections to each of the coordinate planes.

From now on, you will also adopt a more compact notation for specifying the differential equation:

$$(t, x_1, x_2, \ldots, x_n) \rightarrow [f_1, f_2, \ldots, f_n]$$

[1] Hendrick Kooijman, Daniel Schwalbe, and Ross Taylor, "Solving Stiff Differential Equations and Differential Algebraic Systems with Maple V" (submitted to *Maple Technical Newsletter*, 1995).

Note that this notation does not work with **dsolve** because **dsolve** handles more general equations and is not designed to just solve the equations numerically.

Orbit for van der Pol's equation with projections onto coordinate planes.

```
orbitplot(
    (t,x,y)->[10*(y - x^3/3 + x),-0.1*x],
    t = 0..100, x = -3..3, y = -2..2,
    init = [0, 1, 0.7],
    intmethod = besirk, flowcolor = red,
    view = [x,t,y],
    projections = [x = -4, t = 105,y = -3]);
```

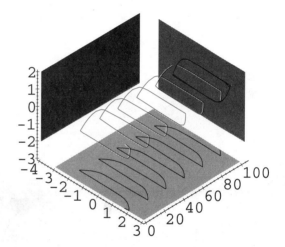

Orbit and projections for van der Pol's equation.

The **projection** option puts a gray rectangle and projection of orbit onto each coordinate plane specified in the list. Thus, in the preceding graph, you have the coordinate planes, $x = -4$, $t = 105$, and $y = -3$. Ranges for the dependent variables are required when asking for projections to the coordinate plane.

orbitplot also works with multiple initial values. Another important option is to view the orbits using the **flowparametricplot** value for the **parametricplot** option. The orbits are then shown with increasing thickness in the direction of the flow. This idea was first used in a book by Leon Glass and Daniel Kaplan.[2] The power of this method of visualization is that one can immediately see not only the direction of flow but also the speed of the flow.

[2] Daniel Kaplan and Leon Glass, *Understanding Nonlinear Dynamics* (New York: Springer, 1995).

The options that control the appearance of the resulting fish-like shapes are **numsteps** and **segments**. The **segments** option controls how many steps are used for each fish. Because **flowparametricplot** does not work as well with variable step-size numerical algorithms, it is generally used with the default algorithm.

The following is a standard example used when studying the Poincaré-Bendixson Theorem.

Example using
flowparametricplot.

```
orbitplot(
    (t,x,y) -> [2*y, 2*x-3*x^2 - 5*y*
    (x^3-x^2+y^2)],
    t = -3..3, x = -2..2, y = -2..2,
    inits = [seq([0, i/4, 0], i = -7..7)],
    numsteps = 200,
    segments = 25, bound = true,
    flowcolor = redscale,
    parametricplot = flowparametricplot,
    background = gray,
    view = [x,y]);
```

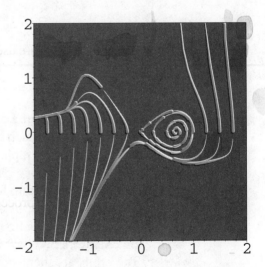

Fish shapes used to visualize flow.

The option **flowcolor** controls the color of the fish and can be either a solid color or a procedure that parameterizes a color scheme on the unit interval. For the purposes of coloring the flow for this manual, a macro called **redscale** was written that colors the fish from white to red.

5.3   Graphical Procedures for First-Order Differential Equations

Direction Fields

Single first-order differential equations can be analyzed using a direction field.

From a geometric point of view, the equation

$$\frac{dy}{dt} = f(t, y)$$

defines the slope of the tangent line at every point in the ty-plane of the solution through that point. You can use Maple to calculate the endpoints of line segments of some fixed length through each point of a grid of points in the ty-plane, and then you can graph these line segments. The resulting graph is called the *direction field* of the differential equation.

The Maple procedure to plot a direction field is **directionfield**.

The Maple procedure used to calculate and plot these line segments is called **directionfield**. This procedure is contained in the **ODE2** file and must be read into the current Maple session before it will work. It requires three arguments and has several optional arguments as follows:

The general form of the **directionfield** procedure is

```
directionfield(f,h,v,<options>);
```

f must be a Maple procedure that defines the right-hand side of the equation, **h** is the horizontal range, and **v** is the vertical range of the grid points for which the line segments are calculated. One possible option is to ask for the zero isoclines with the **nullclines = true** option.

Plot the direction field for the equation dy/dt = t + sin(2y).

```
eq := (t, y) -> t + sin(2*y);
directionfield(eq, t = -2..2, y = -2..2,
    nullclines = true);
```

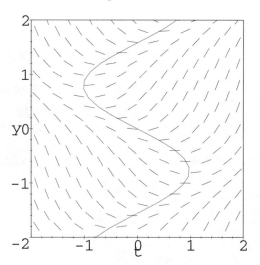

Direction field for
$dy/dt = t + \sin(2y)$.

Notice on the graph that the zero isocline divides the direction field into regions where the slope is positive and the slope is negative.

Maple will not find a closed-form solution for the equation $dy/dt = t + \sin(2y)$. You can, however, use **directionfield** to sketch some approximate solutions. One of the optional arguments for **directionfield** is to specify a set of initial points in a manner similar to the way initial points were done with **orbitplot**. A numerical approximation to the solution through each point is drawn using a fourth-order Runge/Kutta numerical scheme by default. In the context of drawing direction fields, these approximate solutions are referred to as flow lines. Initial conditions are most often generated using Maple's sequence function, **seq**.

You can specify initial conditions for **directionfield**.

```
eq := (t, y) -> t + sin(2*y);
inits := seq([0, i], i = -2..2):
directionfield(eq, t = -2..2, y = -2..2,
   {inits});
```

Now you can see the flow lines that pass through the points given by the initial conditions.

More **directionfield** *options.*

The option for **directionfield** that controls how many grid points are chosen for drawing the direction field is **grid**. An argument such as **grid = [15, 15]** is added to the list of arguments for **directionfield**. To draw a plot that includes flow lines and no line segments of the direction field, just specify **grid=[0,0]**.

In general, the smaller the interval used, the more accurate the approximate solution is. The option for **directionfield** that controls the size of this interval is **stepsize**. An argument such as **stepsize=0.1** is added to the list of arguments for **directionfield**. Alternatively, with the **numsteps** option, you can specify more steps to be taken. An option to decrease the step size is **iterations**. For example, **iterations = 5** decreases the step size by a factor of 5 without plotting more points. The routine is much faster if the step size is decreased using the **iterations** option rather than the **stepsize** option, but then the stored points may be too far apart for a nice plot.

Another possibility, as in the case of **orbitplot**, is to specify a different numerical scheme such as the variable step method **besirk** with the **intmethod = besirk** option.

Adding flow lines to the fieldplot will sometimes give a better indication of what the solutions will look like. Getting the correct step size requires some experimentation, and on a slower machine, it is wise to experiment with a small number of initial values.

Plot the direction field and some flow lines for $dy/dt = -y * \tan(t)$.

```
eq3 := (t, y) -> -y*tan(t);
init3 := {[0,1],[0,2],[0,3],[0,4]}:
directionfield(eq3, t = -6..6, y = -4..4,
    init3, iterations = 5, stepsize = 0.1);
```

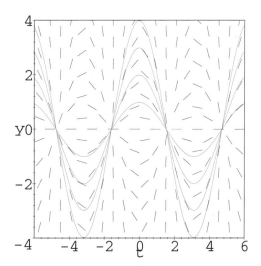

Flow lines for $dy/dt = -y * \tan(t)$.

Every solution approaches 0 as t approaches $\pi/2 + n\pi$ for all integers n, as can be verified by using **dsolve** to find the "exact" solution.

Analysis of equations is necessary to use graphical information.

In some cases, **directionfield** allows you to get a rough idea of what solutions to differential equations will look like. However, there are many parameters and options to set, and in some cases the results will be misleading. Further analysis for some equations is accomplished by considering isoclines. An isocline is a curve in the ty-plane along which the value for dy/dt remains constant or is undefined. Consider the following equation:

$$\frac{dy}{dt} = \frac{y - 3\sin(t)}{t - 2y}.$$

directionfield *with* **besirk** *works well on some nasty equations.*

If you use **directionfield** with the previous values for initial conditions, the resulting plot will be a mess unless you specify **intmethod = besirk**. This is the case because, for $y = t/2$, the function

$$(t, y) = \frac{(y - 3\sin(t))}{(t - 2y)}$$

is undefined. Any solution approaching a point on the line $y = t/2$ is discontinuous, and the Runge/Kutta scheme has no way of detecting this.

The zero isoclines are given by the curve $y = 3\sin(t)$. That is, the slope of the direction field is 0 for any point on this curve. The zero isocline and the undefined isocline break the ty-plane up into several regions. In each region, the function $f(t, y) = (y - 3\sin(t))/(t - 2y)$ is either positive or negative throughout the region.

As you have seen, one way to include the isoclines in a plot is to specify the option **nullclines = true**. This is often unsatisfactory if there are undefined isoclines in the plot. In these cases, a better way is to save the direction field Maple draws as a named plot structure and then have Maple sketch the isoclines in a separate plot. You can then combine the two plot structures using a Maple command called **display**. This command must be read in with the command **with(plots);**. Add a colon at the end of each plot statement to avoid having to watch the entire plot structure scroll across the screen.

Plot the direction field and some isoclines. Note the placement of colons.

```
eq2 := (t, y) -> (y - 3*sin(t))/(t - 2*y);
inits := seq(seq([2*i + 1, 2*j + 1],
   i = -2..1), j= -2..1):
eq2field := directionfield(eq2, t = -5..5,
   y = -5..5, {inits},
   intmethod = besirk):
eq2iso := plot(3*sin(t), t/2,
   t = -5..5, y = -5..5):
plots[display]({eq2field,eq2iso});
```
The graph is shown below.

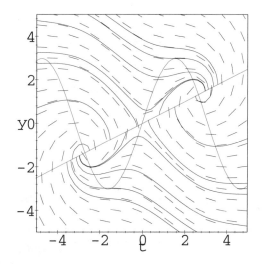

Direction field and some isoclines for
$$dy/dt = \frac{y - 3\sin(t)}{t - 2y}$$

Autonomous equations can be viewed with **phaseline**.

Another graphical view of single first-order equations is possible for the autonomous case. This is where the differential equation does not depend on *t*.

Plot the phase space for the autonomous equation $y' = y(y - 2)$.

```
eq2 := (t, y) -> y*(y-2);
phaseline(eq2, x = -5..5,
   flowfield = true,
   flowcolor = redscale);
```

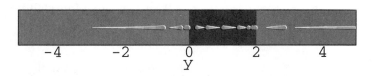

Phase line for
$dy/dt = y(y - 2)$.

Additional Activities

Use the **directionfield** procedure to sketch a direction field for each of the following equations. Find the isoclines for each equation and sketch them by hand or with Maple. Use Maple to sketch some solutions.

1. $dy/dt = -t/y$
2. $dy/dt = \sin(4ty)$
3. $dy/dt = 5y - 6e^{-t}$
4. $dy/dt = t/y$
5. $dy/dt = y(y - 1)(y + 1)$
6. $dy/dt = t + y$
7. $dy/dt = t^2 - y^2$
8. $dy/dt = y + t^2 t$

5.4 Numerical Procedures

Euler's Method

Solutions to differential equations can be approximated.

In "real world" applications of differential equations, solutions are often approximated because closed-form solutions cannot always be found. The simplest way to approximate a solution essentially pieces together the field lines you have already drawn for a differential equation. Consider a differential equation of the form

$$\frac{dy}{dt} = f(t, y), \quad y(t_0) = y_0$$

You can use a numerical algorithm known as Euler's method to approximate solutions to differential equations.

To approximate a solution, calculate the slope of the solution at the initial condition and use this to approximate the solution by a straight line. Then increment t by a fixed amount, calculate the slope of the solution through the resulting point on the line, and then repeat the process. The amount by which t is incremented is called the step size. To a large extent, the step size determines how accurate the approximation is. This algorithm is known as Euler's method. The kth iteration of this process is given by the equations

$$t_{k+1} = t_k + h, \quad y_{k+1} = y_k + hf(t_k, y_k)$$

where h is the step size and $y_0 = y(t_0)$ is the given initial condition.

Maple is a robust programming language specially designed to program mathematics.

If you have had some programming experience, you can see that Euler's method can be easily implemented in many different programming languages. Maple is a simple yet powerful programming language designed to solve mathematics problems. The construction in Maple that is best suited to performing the iterations required by Euler's method is the **for** loop, which you saw in earlier chapters.

Consider the differential equation $dy/dt = \sin(y)$ with the initial condition $y(0) = 1/3$. Use the variables **tk** and **yk** to store the calculations at each step; perform 10 steps with a step size of 0.2.

Use a simple loop in Maple to calculate Euler's method.

```
tk := 0;
yk := evalf(1/3);
for i from 1 to 10
  do
    yk := evalf(yk +.2*sin(yk));
    tk := evalf(tk +.2);
    print(tk,yk);
  od:
```

The colon after the **od** statement (which denotes the end of the **do** statement) suppresses the printing of the calculations as they are executed in the **do** loop. Because Maple does symbolic manipulations, you must use **evalf** to force Maple to do decimal calculations. For this example, some of the **evalf**'s are unnecessary, but it is better to have too many than too few. You may want to try running this example with **evalf** removed from each statement to see for yourself what happens.

It is possible to store the intermediate results in a form in which you can graph them or selectively print out certain values. Maple data structures are flexible and numerous. You will consistently use a data structure known as a **list** to represent a point. For example, the point $(0, 1, -2)$ in three-space would be entered as follows:

A Maple list to represent a point.

```
pt := [0,1,-2];
```

The individual components of the point are then accessed via brackets: **pt[1] = 0**, **pt[2] = 1**, and **pt[3] = -2**. You will use a data structure known, in Maple, as an array to store the points. An array to store the points calculated in the above loop would be declared in the following way:

Declaring an array in Maple.

```
expts := array(0..10);
```
The components of the array are indexed from 0 to 10 and can be accessed via brackets. For example, after filling each component of the array **expts** with a point (that is, by a **list** of numbers), the first point would be accessed as **expts[0]**, and the second component of the fifth point would be accessed as **expts[4][2]**.

It is a good idea and standard programming practice to initialize some variables before running the loop. This makes it easier to modify the example and run it with different parameters.

Use a loop to program Euler's method in Maple for the equation
$dy/dt = y^2 + t^2 - 1$,
$y(-2) = -2$, *with 20 iterations of step size* 0.2.

```
ex := (t,y) -> y^2+t^2-1;
h := 0.2;
n := 20;
tk := -2.0;
yk := -2.0;
expts := array(0..n);
expts[0] := [tk,yk];
for i from 1 to n
   do
      yk:=evalf(yk+h*ex(tk,yk));
      tk:=tk+h;
      expts[i] := [tk,yk];
   od:
print(expts);
```
To plot the points stored in the array **expts**, the array must be converted to a list. This is accomplished with a Maple command called **makelist**.

You can also plot the points stored in the array **expts**.

```
plot({makelist(expts)});
```

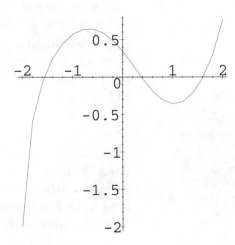

Approximation to the solution for
$dy/dt = y^2 + t^2 - 1$,
$y(-2) = -2$ *using Euler's method with step size of* 0.2.

Storing the points in an array also provides the advantage of allowing you to access each point using the selection operation for arrays. To print out the last value for *y*, which in this case represents the approximation to *y*(2), enter

Print out the approximate value for y(2).

```
expts[20][2];
```

To see how accurate this approximation is, reenter the commands with a smaller step size, larger number of iterations, and a *different* name for the array to store the points. You can then subtract the two approximate values to get an idea of how many decimal places of accuracy you have.

Rerun the loop for dy/dt = $y^2 + t^2 - 1$, $y(-2) = -2$, with 40 iterations and a step size of 0.1.

```
ex := (t,y) -> y^2+t^2-1;
h := 0.1;
n := 40;
tk := -2.0;
yk := -2.0;
expts2 := array(0..n);
expts2[0] := [tk,yk];
for i from 1 to n
   do
      yk:=evalf(yk+h*ex(tk,yk));
      tk:=tk+h;
      expts2[i] := [tk,yk];
   od:
print(expts[20][2]-expts2[40][2]);
```

The difference is displayed. Better yet, you can visualize what the change in step size does by plotting both arrays on the same graph along with the direction field. You must use two plot structures, one for the direction field and one for the points you calculated. They are then combined with the **display** command. Remember to use a colon at the end of the plot statements.

Plot the output of the Euler method with different step sizes.

```
exfield:= directionfield(ex,t = -2..2,
   y = -2..2):
exrkplot:=plot({makelist(expts),
             makelist(expts2)}):
plots[display](exfield, exrkplot);
```

The graph makes it clear that the small difference between the two approximations at *t* = 2 is deceiving.

Additional Activities

1. Use Euler's method with a step size of $h = 0.1$ to determine an approximate value of the solution at $t = 1$ for each of the initial value problems a–e. Repeat these computations with $h = 0.05$ and $h = 0.025$ and compare the results with the actual value of $y(1)$. Graph the results along with the direction field in each case.

   a. $dy/dt = y, y(0) = 1$
   b. $dy/dt = y + t, y(0) = 1$
   c. $dy/dt = t - y, y(0) = 1$
   d. $dy/dt = 5y - 6e^{-t}, y(0) = 1$
   e. $dy/dt = 25y(1 - y), y(0) = 1.3$

2. Use Euler's method with 10, 20, and 40 iterations to determine an approximate value of the solution at the indicated value of t for each of the initial value problems a and b. Graph the results along with the direction field in each case.

   a. $dy/dt = \sin(4ty), y(\sqrt{\pi/2}) = \sqrt{\pi}/2, t = \sqrt{\pi}$ (Use the built-in Maple expression **evalf(Pi)** for the value of π.)
   b. $dy/dt = y^2, y(0) = 1, t = 1$

Improved Euler Method

Euler's method can be improved so as to yield a numerical scheme known as the Improved Euler method. It is similar to Euler's method in that it is a one-step method, but the error is proportional to h^2, where h is the step size. The iterates for $dy/dt = f(t, y), y(t_0) = y_0$ are given by the formula

$$t_{k+1} = t_k + h$$
$$y_{k+1} = y_k + \frac{h}{2}(f(t_k, y_k) + f(t_k + h, y_k + hf(t_k, y_k)))$$

Adapting the previous loop to implement this method is simple.

Adapt the previous loop to use the Improved Euler method.

```
ex := (t,y) -> y^2+t^2-1;
h := 0.2;
n := 20;
tk := -2;
yk := -2;
```

```
expts3 := array(0..n);
expts3[0] := [tk,yk];
for i from 1 to n
  do
    yk:=evalf(yk+h/2*(ex(tk,yk)+
            ex(tk+h,yk+h*ex(tk,yk))));
    tk:=tk+h;
    expts3[i] := [tk,yk];
  od:
print(expts3);
```

Runge/Kutta Method

Runge/Kutta is a highly accurate numerical method often used by professional engineers.

Many numerical schemes have been developed. One of the most popular is a fourth-order Runge/Kutta method. A Maple procedure to perform the calculations is contained in the **ODE2** file.

The error in Runge/Kutta is proportional to h^4, which results in a rapid decrease in errors when the step size is reduced. Due to the accuracy of the method and the fact that each step requires multiple calculations, we must be careful that round-off errors do not become significant, especially for very small step sizes. You will explore this facet of the method at the end of this section.

The **ODE2** *file contains implementations of different numerical schemes for approximating solutions to initial value problems.*

The Euler and Improved Euler methods have also been implemented in Maple procedures. These procedures are called **firsteuler**, **impeuler**, and **rungekutta**. Each of these procedures requires four arguments: the name of a Maple procedure that defines the right-hand side of the differential equation, a list of numbers for the initial condition, the step size, and the number of steps to be taken.

Code to use Runge/Kutta to estimate the solution to the differential equation $dy/dt = y$, $y(0) = 1$ for $0 \le t \le 1$.

```
eq := (t, y) -> y;
eqrkpts := rungekutta(eq, [0, 1], 0.2, 5);
```

which returns the following:

```
eqrkpts := array(0 .. 5,, [
                0 = [0, 1.]
                1 = [.2, 1.221399999]
                2 = [.4, 1.491817958]
                3 = [.6, 1.822106454]
```

```
        4 = [.8,  2.225520824]
        5 = [1.0,  2.718251135]
    ])
```

The exact solution to the problem $dy/dt = y$, $y(0) = 1$ is $y(t) = e^t$. You see that the error is already very small with only five iterations.

Calculate the error in Runge/Kutta with five iterations.

```
evalf(eqrkpts[5][2]-exp(1));
```

We will end this section with an example to highlight the capabilities of Maple and to explore the possibility of round-off errors in the calculations. Return to the problem $dy/dt = y$, $y(0) = 1$. The solution to this equation is $y(t) = e^t$. Estimate the value $y(1)$ using step sizes of 0.1, 0.01, and 0.001 for each method and compare this estimate with the known value of e. With a step size of 0.001, you would be storing 1000 points and you are only interested in looking at the last point. An optional fifth argument to each routine decreases the step size without storing more points. For example, a 10 in the fifth spot decreases the step size by a factor of 10, and only every tenth point is stored in the array. So, for each example, you can put a 1 in the third and fourth spots and change the fifth spot appropriately to do more iterations. The calculations are performed as follows:

Compare the output of the numerical methods for the equation
$dy/dt = y$, $y(0) = 1$
for the value $y(1)$.

```
Digits := 20;
ex := (t,y) -> y;
eu1 := firsteuler(ex,[0,1],1,1,10):
eu2 := firsteuler(ex,[0,1],1,1,100):
eu3 := firsteuler(ex,[0,1],1,1,1000):
im1 := impeuler(ex,[0,1],1,1,10):
im2 := impeuler(ex,[0,1],1,1,100):
im3 := impeuler(ex,[0,1],1,1,1000):
rk1 := rungekutta(ex,[0,1],1,1,10):
rk2 := rungekutta(ex,[0,1],1,1,100):
rk3 := rungekutta(ex,[0,1],1,1,1000):
e := evalf(exp(1));
print('euler, impeuler, rungekutta');
print(e-eu1[1][2],
        e-im1[1][2],
        e-rk1[1][2]);
print(e-eu2[1][2],
        e-im2[1][2],
        e-rk2[1][2]);
```

```
print(e-eu3[1][2],
      e-im3[1][2],
      e-rk3[1][2]);
```

The output of these print statements is the following:

Errors in Euler, Improved Euler, and Runge/Kutta for step sizes of 0.1, 0.01, and 0.001.

```
euler,    impeuler, rungekutta
                                    -5
.12453,    .00420,       .20843 10
                                    -9
.01346,    .00004,       .22464 10
                       -6          -13
.00135,    .45270 10,    .22632 10
```

The calculations were run with 20 digits of accuracy, for, as you can see, the **rungekutta** command with a step size of 0.1 is already accurate to 9 digits. You see that for the Euler method you get one more decimal place of accuracy each time h is divided by 10, and for the Improved Euler method you get two more decimal places of accuracy each time. The Runge/Kutta scheme resulted in four more decimal places of accuracy for each division of h by 10.

The **rungekutta** procedure is accurate to 5 significant digits with just 10 iterations on this problem. To get this same accuracy with **firsteuler** would require around a million iterations.

Numerical Methods for Systems

Numerical methods for a system of first-order differential equations are no harder to implement than those for a single first-order equation. However, the points are generated for higher-dimensional coordinate systems. A fourth-order Runge/Kutta scheme is used to get the orbits in the **directionfield** procedure by default. You can use the **rungekutta** and **besirk** procedures to estimate solutions to systems of equations. You can use essentially the same syntax as for **orbitplot**. In fact, if you are interested only in the graphs and not the actual points, it is probably best to use **orbitplot**. A call to **besirk** for a system of two first-order equations might look like the following:

```
diffeq := (t,x,y) ->
               [f(t,x,y),g(t,x,y)];
besirk(diffeq,[t0, x0, y0],t = ti..tf):
```

This procedure would return an array. Each array entry contains a list of three numbers, which represents a point in three-space. You can plot these points two coordinates at a time using a Maple procedure called **makelist**, which is written **makelist(A,m,n)**, where **A** is an array of lists of numbers and **m** and **n** are integers that denote the position of the coordinates you wish to plot. For example, **makelist(A,2,3)** will pick out the second and third coordinates of each point in the array **A**. Consider the following pair of second-order equations. They represent a double pendulum—that is, a pendulum attached to a pendulum.

$$\theta_1'' = -2\sin(\theta_1) + \sin(\theta_2)$$
$$\theta_2'' = -2\sin(\theta_2) + 2\sin(\theta_1)$$

You can translate this into a system of four first-order equations using the variables $x = \theta_1$, $xp = \theta_1'$, $y = \theta_2$, and $yp = \theta_2'$. Assume the pendulums start at rest and the bottom pendulum is given a push of $\frac{1}{2}$ unit/second.

Solve the double-pendulum equations.

```
dp := (t,x,xp,y,yp)->
      [xp, -2*sin(x) + sin(y),
       yp, -2*sin(y) + 2*sin(x)];
dpinit := [0, 0 ,0, 0, 1/2];
dppts := besirk(dp, dpinit, t = 0..30,
      numpoints = 300):
```

The colon at the end of the **besirk** statement suppresses the printing of all 300 points. By default, **besirk** calculates very few points, as it is very efficient. But for nice-looking graphs you need to ask for more points. In some cases, you will want to look at the array of points generated; to do so, you can add a print statement. In fact, if you only want a plot, you can accomplish this with **orbitplot**, as we saw in section 5.2. Here you look at a plot of the approximate solution for θ_1 versus θ_2.

Plot the second and fourth coordinates.

```
plot({makelist(dppts, 2, 4)});
```

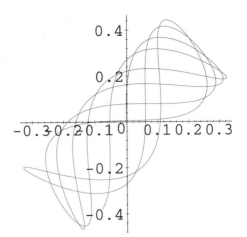

A plot of the solution to the system for θ_1 versus θ_2 generated using **rungekutta**.

Additional Activities

1. Use the **rungekutta** procedure with a step size of $h = 0.1$ to determine an approximate value of the solution at $t = 1$ for each of the initial value problems a–d. Repeat these computations with $h = 0.05$ and $h = 0.025$ and compare the results with the actual value. Graph the results along with the direction field in each case.

   a. $dy/dt = y$, $y(0) = 1$
   b. $dy/dt = y + t$, $y(0) = 1$
   c. $dy/dt = t - y$, $y(0) = 1$
   d. $dy/dt = 5y - 6e^{-t}$, $y(0) = 1$

2. A conical tank is 12 meters deep, and its open top has a radius of 12 meters. Initially the tank is empty. Water is added at a rate of 3 meters^3/hour. Water evaporates at a rate proportional to the surface area of the water. The constant of proportionality is 0.01 meter/hour. Use **rungekutta** to estimate the height of the water to one decimal place accuracy after 100 hours. Plot the depth of the water for the first 100 hours. Find the time at which the tank has 6 meters of water in it. To get a starting value for **rungekutta**, assume the evaporation is negligible for the first half-hour.

3. A mass–spring–dashpot system is governed by the second-order equation $my'' + cy' + ky = 0$, where m is the mass, c is the damping constant, and k is the spring constant. Use

rungekutta to draw the solutions to the equation in the yy'-plane for $k = 1$, $m = 1$, and $c = 0, 0.5, 1.0, 1.5, 2$. Use $y'(0) = 1$, $y(0) = 0$ for your initial values and do 30 iterations with a step size of 0.5 for each.

4. A ball of mass 1 gram is thrown into the air with an initial velocity of 10 meters/second. Assuming air resistance proportional to velocity with constant of proportionality 2.0, use **rungekutta** to find the maximum height of the ball and the velocity of the ball when it hits the ground. The height of the ball satisfies the second-order equation

$$my'' = -mg - ry'$$

assuming that upward is the positive direction.

5. Use the same setup as in Activity 4, only assume air resistance is proportional to velocity squared with constant of proportionality 0.2. For positive velocity the equation is

$$my'' = -mg - r(y')^2$$

and for negative velocity the equation is

$$my'' = -mg + r(y')^2$$

Plot position versus time for the cases where air resistance is proportional to velocity and velocity squared and the case where it is ignored.

6. A long, heavy string is attached to a balloon filled with helium. The motion of the balloon is governed by Newton's equation, which gives

$$\frac{d}{dt}(mv) = mg + H + R + G$$

where y is the height of the balloon above the ground, m is the mass of the part of the string that is above the ground (and is thus a function of position), H is the force of helium on the balloon, R is the force of air resistance, G is the force of the ground on the rope, and g is the gravitational constant. Suppose that ρ is the linear density of the string so that $m = \rho y$; $R = \lambda v$ is the force of air resistance, where λ is the resistance coefficient; and y_e is the equilibrium position of the balloon (that is, $H = y_e \rho g$).

The force of the ground is given by $G = \rho v^2$. Note that this force applies only for the system when the balloon is falling.

Consider the situation where $g = 9.8$ meters/second^2, $\rho = 0.25$ kilograms/meter, $\lambda = 0.03$ kilograms/second, and $y_e = 2.0$ meters. Use the Maple procedure **rungekutta** to predict the highest point the balloon will reach and the time at which it will reach this height.

7. If the ball in Activity 4 also has a horizontal position denoted by x, and assuming the air resistance is proportional to velocity directed opposite to its instantaneous direction of motion, you get the following equations:

$$mx'' = -rx'\sqrt{(x')^2 + (y')^2}$$
$$my'' = -ry'\sqrt{(x')^2 + (y')^2} - mg$$

Assume a trajectory of 45 degrees, initial velocity of 10 meters/second, and coefficient of resistance of 2. Use the procedure **rungekutta** to find the maximum height of the ball, the time when the ball hits the ground, and the horizontal distance traveled. Compare these quantities with the flight of the ball without air resistance. Plot the solution in the xy-plane with and without air resistance.

8. An iron mass is attached to a spring and is suspended above a magnet. The spring exerts a force on the iron mass proportional to the distance the spring is stretched/compressed from its natural length, with proportionality constant κ. The magnet exerts a force inversely proportional to the distance between the iron mass and the magnet with proportionality constant μ. Taking $y = 0$ to be the position of the mass when the spring force is equal to the weight of the mass and taking d to be the distance to the magnet from this position, derive the following equation:

$$my'' = -\kappa y + \frac{\mu}{d - y}$$

Using the values $m = 1$, $\kappa = 1$, $\mu = 20$, and $d = 10$, use **rungekutta** to sketch the motion for y versus v if the mass is pulled down to $y = 7$ and released.

5.5 Phase Space

The goal in this section is to get some qualitative (graphical) information for systems of two first-order equations.

A general system of two first-order equations can be written as follows:

$$\frac{dx_1}{dt} = f_1(t, x_1, x_2) \tag{5.2}$$

$$\frac{dx_2}{dt} = f_2(t, x_1, x_2) \tag{5.3}$$

Solutions are curves in three-dimensional space.

Solutions to system of equations (5.2) and (5.3) parametrically describe a curve in three-space. This solution curve is the set of points $(t, x_1(t), x_2(t))$ as t ranges over some interval for which the solution is defined. Consider the system of equations:

$$x_1' = x_2, \ x_2' = -x_1 - \frac{1}{2}x_2, \ x_1(0) = 0, \ x_2(0) = 1$$

Solve the system of equations and plot a solution curve.

```
deq1 := D(x1)(t) = x2(t);
deq2 := D(x2)(t) = -x1(t) - x2(t)/2;
deqinit := x1(0) = 0, x2(0) = 1;
deqsol := dsolve({deq1, deq2, deqinit},
   {x1(t), x2(t)});
plots[spacecurve](subs(deqsol,[t, x1(t),
   x2(t)]), t = 0..20,  axes = NORMAL);
```

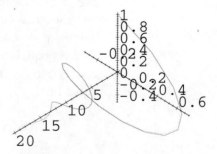

Solution curve plotted with **spacecurve** *command.*

You can see from the plot that this solution is approaching the t-axis as t goes to infinity. That is, both x_1 and x_2 are approaching 0 for this curve.

Direction fields are not practical for three-dimensional systems.

The analog of the direction field you drew for one equation would be three-dimensional and would be rather difficult to visualize on a two-dimensional computer screen. As it turns out, many physically interesting differential equations are independent of time; that is, f_1 and f_2 in equations (5.2) and (5.3) do not depend on the t variable. These are known as *autonomous differential equations*.

   For a system of two autonomous first-order equations, $x' = f(x, y)$, $y' = g(x, y)$, the direction of flow from each point in the xy-plane is independent of time. You can thus picture the flow of the solutions in the xy-plane by plotting a vector in the direction of flow at every point on a grid. Alternatively, you can plot a short segment of the flow for many points in the plane to get an overall picture of the flow. This flow picture is enhanced by the ideas of Kaplan and Glass, which you used in section 5.2, to randomly pick the points of flow and indicate the direction of flow by increasing the width of the flow.

*The **phaseplot** procedure calculates flows and orbits.*

A procedure in the **ODE2** file called **phaseplot** will do either of these tasks. The default is to draw vectors on a grid. The **flowfield = true** option randomly places fish shapes to indicate the flow. The resulting picture is referred to as a phase portrait of the system.

Plot the flow for a system.

```
eq := (t ,x1, x2) -> [x/5 + x2, -x - x2/2];
phaseplot(eq, x = -2..2, x2 = -2..2,
    flowfield = true);
```

Phase portrait of
$x' = x_1/5 + x_2$
$y' = -x_1 - x_2/2$

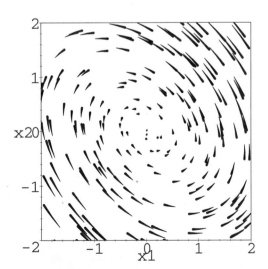

The phase portrait for this system is similar to the direction field of the first-order differential equation

$$\frac{dx_2}{dx_1} = \frac{-x_1 - x_2/2}{x_1/5 + x_2}$$

Lines tangent to the flow will be equal to the slopes of the line segments of the direction field.

You can combine this graph with a plot of the orbit of the solution you found in the first example in this section. You must be careful to plot x_1 along the horizontal axis and x_2 along the vertical axis if that is the order the variables were specified for the **phaseplot** command.

Plot the solution you found earlier along with the phase vectors.

```
orb1 := plot(subs(deqsol, [x1(t), x2(t),
    t = 0..20]), x1 = -1..1, x2 = -1..1):
phasevects := phaseplot(eq,
    x1 = -1..1, x2 = -1..1):
plots[display]({orb1, phasevects});
```

Compare this with the **spacecurve** you plotted earlier. By rotating the earlier solution curve appropriately, you can make it match the picture of the orbit in the phase portrait.

phaseplot *can be used to plot orbits.*

For many examples, a closed-form solution cannot be found. **phaseplot** has a facility for plotting orbits that is similar to the way in which **directionfield** was able to approximate solutions using the Runge/Kutta numerical method or the **besirk** numerical method if specified. The options to **phaseplot** are similar to **directionfield** or **orbitplot** in that initial points can be specified for orbits, and the options **grid**, **iterations**, **numsteps**, and **stepsize** are implemented in the same way.

Consider the following second-order equation, which comes from Newton's second law of motion for a pendulum with friction:

$$\frac{dy^2}{d^2t} = -\sin(y) - 0.2\frac{dy}{dt}$$

where y is the radian measure of the pendulum from the bottom position. This leads to a system of two first-order equations:

$$dy/dt = v$$
$$dv/dt = -\sin(y) - 0.2v$$

In the following, you ask Maple to sketch the nullclines, which are the curves $y' = 0$ and $v' = 0$. This breaks the plot into regions where the signs of y' and v' do not change, so that in each region the flow is up and to the right, up and to the left, down and to the right, or down and to the left. You also use some of the fancy color options that were introduced with **orbitplot**.

Plot some orbits and the nullclines for the pendulum-with-friction equations.

```
pend := (t,y,v) -> [v, -sin(y) - 0.4*v];
pendinits := seq(seq([0, 2*i, 2*j],
   i= 0..2), j= -2..2):
phaseplot(pend, y = -3..10, v = -6..6,
   t = -2 .. 15, {pendinits},
   parametricplot = flowparametricplot,
   flowcolor = redscale,
   numsteps=200, segments = 25,
   nullclines = true,
   vectorfield = false,
   background = gray);
```

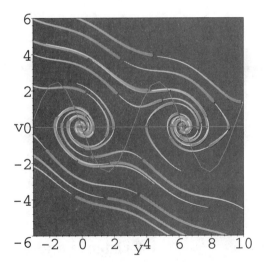

Phase portrait and orbits for pendulum equations.

The points $(n\pi, 0)$ for any integer n are points where the phase vectors have length 0; these are called equilibrium points. From this, you can see that any solution that comes near the points $(2n\pi, 0)$ tends to approach these points. The points $((2n + 1)\pi, 0)$ are unstable equilibrium points. The study of equilibrium points is an important topic in the theory of autonomous systems. Phase portraits are a good tool to help understand these and other important characteristics of autonomous systems.

Additional Activities

1. Transform each of equations a–e into a system of two first-order equations by making the substitution $v = dy/dt$. Use Maple's **phaseplot** procedure to draw a phase portrait for each equation. In each case, find the regions in which dy/dt and dv/dt are positive and negative, and compare this information with the phase portraits drawn by Maple.

   a. $y'' + y' - 2y = 0$
   b. $y'' - 3y' + 2y = 0$
   c. $y'' - 2y' + y = 0$
   d. $y'' - 2y' + 2y = 0$
   e. $y'' - 2y' - 2y = 0$

2. For each of equations a–e, use Maple to draw a phase portrait. For each equilibrium point, decide whether the nearby orbits are approaching the equilibrium point.

   a. $x' = y^2 - x^2,\ y' = x - 2y$
   b. $x' = y^2 - x^2,\ y' = x - \sin(y)$
   c. $x' = \sin(y) - x,\ y' = \cos(x) - y$
   d. $x' = y^2 + x^2 - 4,\ y' = y^2 - x^2$
   e. $x' = \sin(2*x) - y,\ y' = \cos(2*x) - y$

5.6 Picard Iterates

The following theorem is the cornerstone in the study of differential equations.

Existence and Uniqueness Theorem

Let f and $\partial f/\partial y$ be continuous in some neighborhood of (t_0, y_0). Then the initial value problem

$$\frac{dy}{dt} = f(t, y), \quad y(t_0) = y_0$$

has a unique solution on some open interval containing t_0.

The usual proof of this theorem involves constructing a sequence of functions, known as the Picard iterates of the equation, and showing that they always converge to a solution on some interval containing t_0. The Picard iterates are inductively defined by the equations

$$y_1(t) \;=\; y_0 + \int_{t_0}^{t} f(s, y_0)\, ds$$
$$y_2(t) \;=\; y_0 + \int_{t_0}^{t} f(s, y_1(s))\, ds$$
$$\vdots \qquad\qquad \vdots$$
$$y_{n+1}(t) \;=\; y_0 + \int_{t_0}^{t} f(s, y_n(s))\, ds$$

You can use Maple to see how these iterates converge. As you saw in Chapter 3, Maple can compute definite integrals with an indeterminant upper bound, as is needed to compute the Picard iterates. Consider the initial value problem $y' = \sin(t) + y^2$, $y(0) = 1$.

Compute the first three Picard iterates of $y' = \sin(t) + y^2$, $y(0) = 1$.

```
y0 := 1;
pic1 := y0 + int(sin(s) + y0^2, s = 0..t);
pic2 := y0 + int(sin(s) +
   subs(t = s, pic1)^2, s = 0..t);
pic3 := y0 + int(sin(s) +
   subs(t = s, pic2)^2, s = 0..t);
```

Notice that each Picard iterate is an expression in t. You need to substitute this same expression for y in the differential equation, with s as the independent variable.

A Maple procedure called **picard**, which is built into the **ODE2** file, makes computing and plotting several Picard iterates very easy. It requires three arguments: the procedure name that describes the differential equation, an initial point, and the number of iterates to be computed.

Compute and plot the first five Picard iterates and the solution for $y' = -\dfrac{3y}{t+1}$, $y(0) = 1$

```
diffeq := (t, y) -> -3*y/(t + 1);
diffeqsol := dsolve({diff(y(t), t)=
   diffeq(t, y(t)), y(0) = 1}, y(t));
iterates := picard(diffeq, [0, 1], 5);
plot({rhs(diffeqsol), iterates},
   t = 0..3, y = -2..2);
```

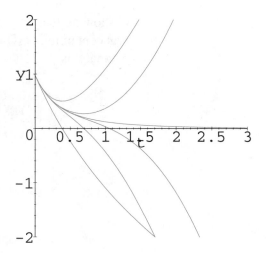

The solution and the first five Picard iterates.

By looking at the form of the solution, you can clearly see which curve corresponds to the solution because the solution approaches zero as t goes to infinity. Each succeeding iterate is closer to the solution for a longer time.

Additional Activities

1. Use the Maple procedure **picard** to compute the first five Picard iterates for the initial value problem

$$y' = y, \ y(0) = 1$$

By hand, find the general formula for the nth Picard iterate and verify that the Picard iterates converge to the solution.

2. Use the Maple procedure **picard** to compute the first five Picard iterates for the initial value problem

$$y' = y/t, \ y(1) = 1$$

Plot these expression along with the solution $y(t) = t$. By hand, find the general formula for the nth Picard iterate. Are the Picard iterates converging to the solution? This example shows clearly why the Picard iterates are not generally a practical method for analyzing differential equations.

5.7 Higher-Order Equations and Systems

Maple's **dsolve** command will recognize and solve many higher-order differential equations. You first need to know how to translate equations into Maple format. To represent the second derivative you use **(D@@2)**, for the third derivative you use **(D@@3)**, and so on. It is also possible to use **diff(y(t),t,t)** and **diff(y(t),t,t,t)** to represent these derivatives. Because **diff** can be used to differentiate expressions, this will be the preferred notation in some cases. Following are a few examples.

Solve the equation
$y'' + 2y' + 3y = 0.$

```
deq1 := (D@@2)(y)(t) + 2*D(y)(t) +
    3*y(t) = 0;
deq1sol := dsolve(deq1, y(t));
```
The solution returned has two constants, **_C1** and **_C2**, as expected. The form of the solution should also be familiar to you if you have studied second-order linear homogeneous differential equations with constant coefficients.

Solve the equation
$t^2y'' + ty' + (t^2 - 1)y = 0.$

```
deq2 := t^2*(D@@2)(y)(t) + t*D(y)(t) +
    (t^2 - 1)*y(t) = 0;
deq2sol:=dsolve(deq2, y(t));
```
The solution is given in terms of two special functions, which are built into Maple. These functions are defined in terms of series, and you will explore these a little more later.

Solve the equation
$yy'' + (y')^2 + y' + 1 = 0.$

```
deq3 := y(t)*(D@@2)(y)(t) + (D(y)(t))^2 +
    D(y)(t) + 1 = 0;
deq3sol := dsolve(deq3, y(t));
```
When Maple cannot solve a differential equation, it will just return the empty string unless it believes the equation was improperly entered. You will be able to use numerical methods to get approximate solutions to many equations that cannot be solved in closed form.

Initial value problems of higher order can also be solved.

Maple's **dsolve** command will also solve initial value problems of higher degrees. The **D** operator is used to specify the initial conditions, as follows.

Solve the initial value problem
$y'' + 2y' + 3y = \sin(t)$
$y(0) = 1/4$
$y'(0) = -1/4$

```
deq4 := (D@@2)(y)(t) + 2*D(y)(t) +
    3*y(t) = sin(t);
deq4init := y(0) = 1/4, D(y)(0) = -1/4 ;
deq4sol := dsolve({deq4, deq4init}, y(t));
```

If you work this problem by hand using the method of undetermined coefficients for constant coefficient equations, you will get a much simpler looking answer. The answers are the same but Maple uses a different algorithm to come up with a solution.

Maple's **dsolve** can also solve systems of differential equations. The equations are specified in Maple as an expression sequence; that is, they are separated by commas.

Solve the system

$$\frac{dx1}{dt} = -x2$$

$$\frac{dx2}{dt} = x1$$

```
sys := D(x1)(t) =-x2(t),
        D(x2)(t) = x1(t);
sol:= dsolve({sys}, {x1(t), x2(t)});
```

Maple returns a set of equations as the solution. The expressions that define the solutions can be obtained by using the **subs** functions: **subs(sol, x1(t))** and **subs(sol, x2(t))**.

Let us solve a system of equations with initial values.

```
sys2 := D(x)(t) = y(t),D(y)(t) =
   -16*x(t) + sin(5*t);
init2 := x(0) = 0, y(0) = 1;
sol2 := dsolve({sys2, init2}, {x(t), y(t)});
```

A pair of equations is returned. There are several interesting graphs to consider for solutions to systems of equations.

Plot x versus t and y versus t for the preceding example.

```
plot({subs(sol2, x(t)), subs(sol2, y(t))},
   t = 0..4*Pi);
```

The two curves correspond to graphs of $x(t)$ and $y(t)$. In particular applications, a parametric plot of $x(t)$ versus $y(t)$ will give you further insight into the system.

Plot a parametric plot of x(t) versus y(t) for the preceding example.

```
plot([subs(sol2, x(t)), subs(sol2, y(t)),
   t=0..2*Pi]);
```

Compare this graph with the previous graph. The set of points in three-space of the form $(t, x(t), y(t))$ for t ranging over some interval is referred to as a solution curve of the system. The three curves you just plotted all give different views of a particular solution curve. Maple has another command, called **spacecurve**, with which to plot still more views of a curve in three-space. It is contained in the **plots** package. The notation is similar to a two-dimensional parametric plot.

Plot a solution curve in three-space.

```
plots[spacecurve](subs(sol2,[t,x(t),y(t)]),
   t=0..4*Pi, axes=FRAME, numpoints=150);
```

By using the three-dimensional options, you can rotate this curve into any of the three other views you have already plotted.

Homogeneous Linear Systems with Constant Coefficients

Maple's built-in linear algebra package can be useful in solving linear systems with constant coefficients.

An important special case of systems of differential equations are linear homogeneous systems with constant coefficients. Many physical systems are modeled by linear systems. More importantly, the study of stability of general systems of equations is based on the stability of constant coefficient, linear, homogeneous systems that have the following form:

$$\frac{dx_1}{dt} = a_{11}x_1 + a_{12}x_2 + \cdots + a_{1n}x_n$$

$$\frac{dx_2}{dt} = a_{21}x_1 + a_{22}x_2 + \cdots + a_{2n}x_n$$

$$\vdots \qquad \qquad \vdots$$

$$\frac{dx_n}{dt} = a_{n1}x_1 + a_{n2}x_2 + \cdots + a_{nn}x_n$$

It is advantageous to adopt a more compact notation that lends itself to the type of calculations you will perform on the system. The notation is adopted from Chapter 4, on linear algebra.

$$\mathbf{x}(t) = \begin{bmatrix} x_1(t) \\ x_2(t) \\ \vdots \\ x_n(t) \end{bmatrix}, \quad \mathbf{A} = \begin{bmatrix} a_{11} & a_{12} & \cdots & a_{1n} \\ a_{21} & a_{22} & \cdots & a_{2n} \\ \vdots & \vdots & & \vdots \\ a_{n1} & a_{n2} & \cdots & a_{nn} \end{bmatrix}$$

With this notation, the system of differential equations is written:

$$\mathbf{x}' = \mathbf{A}\mathbf{x}$$

A solution is now given by a vector-valued function. The set of components of a vector-valued solution will be a solution to the original system. Two theorems from the theory of linear homogeneous systems with constant coefficients are needed.

Existence and Uniqueness Theorem for Linear Homogeneous Systems

There exists one, and only one, solution of the initial value problem

$$\mathbf{x}' = \mathbf{A}\mathbf{x}, \quad \mathbf{x}(t_0) = \mathbf{x}^0 = \begin{bmatrix} x_1^0 \\ x_2^0 \\ \vdots \\ x_n^0 \end{bmatrix}$$

and this solution exists for $-\infty < t < \infty$.

Vector Space Theorem for Linear Homogeneous Systems

The solutions to a system of n homogeneous linear differential equations with constant coefficients form a vector space of dimension n.

These are very important results. They allow you to search for solutions to the system and give you a criterion for knowing when that search is complete. You begin the search by looking for solutions of the form $\mathbf{x}(t) = e^{\lambda t}\mathbf{v}$, where $\mathbf{v}$ is a constant vector. Observe that

$$\frac{d}{dt}\left(e^{\lambda t}\mathbf{v}\right) = \lambda e^{\lambda t}\mathbf{v}$$

and

$$\mathbf{A}(e^{\lambda t}\mathbf{v}) = e^{\lambda t}\mathbf{A}\mathbf{v}$$

It follows that $\mathbf{x}(t) = e^{\lambda t}\mathbf{v}$ is a solution if and only if

$$e^{\lambda t}\mathbf{A}\mathbf{v} = \lambda e^{\lambda t}\mathbf{v}$$

After dividing by $e^{\lambda t}$, you find that λ and $\mathbf{v}$ must satisfy the equation $\mathbf{A}\mathbf{v} = \lambda\mathbf{v}$. Recall that in this case $\mathbf{v}$ is known as the eigenvector associated to the eigenvalue λ for the matrix $\mathbf{A}$. Also, recall that λ is a root of the characteristic polynomial of $\mathbf{A}$. The eigenspace of λ is the subspace of all the eigenvectors associated to λ. You saw in Chapter 4, on linear algebra, that Maple has a built-in facility for finding eigenvectors and eigenvalues of matrices. Refer back to Chapter 4 for the discussion on how to enter matrices and find eigenvalues and eigenvectors in Maple.

Consider the following example:

$$\mathbf{x}' = \begin{pmatrix} 1 & -1 & 4 \\ 3 & 2 & -1 \\ 2 & 1 & -1 \end{pmatrix} \mathbf{x} \tag{5.4}$$

Use Maple to find the eigenvectors of the matrix.

```
with(linalg):
A := matrix(3, 3, [1, -1, 4,
                   3, 2, -1,
                   2, 1, -1]);
eigsA := eigenvects(A);
```

In this case, Maple returns the following sequence of three lists:

```
eigsA := [1, 1, [ -1, 4, 1 ]],
         [-2, 1, [ -1, 1, 1 ]],
         [3, 1, [ 1, 2, 1 ]]
```

Recall that the first component of each list is an eigenvalue, the second component is the multiplicity of the eigenvalue for the characteristic polynomial of **A**, and the third component is a set of eigenvectors that span the eigenspace of the eigenvalue. In this case, you found three eigenvalues, each with an eigenspace of dimension 1. From a basic theorem of advanced linear algebra, we know that the three eigenvectors are linearly independent. It thus follows that the solutions constructed from the three eigenvalues will be linearly independent. Therefore, by the vector space theorem, you can construct the general solution from these three solutions.

Obtain the general solution to equation (5.4).

```
solA := evalm(
   C1*exp(eigsA[1][1]*t)*eigsA[1][3][1] +
   C2*exp(eigsA[2][1]*t)*eigsA[2][3][1] +
   C3*exp(eigsA[3][1]*t)*eigsA[3][3][1]);
```

You can compare this solution with the solution generated by Maple's **dsolve** operator.

Find the general solution to equation (5.4) using **dsolve**.

```
eq1 := D(x1)(t) = x1(t)-x2(t)+4*x3(t);
eq2 := D(x2)(t) = 3*x1(t)+2*x2(t)-x3(t);
eq3 := D(x3)(t) = 2*x1(t)+x2(t)-x3(t);
dsolve({eq1, eq2, eq3},
   {x1(t), x2(t), x3(t)});
```

The answers look different, but you should be able to verify they do indeed give the same general solution.

Complex eigenvalues complicate matters somewhat.

If λ is a complex eigenvalue with complex eigenvector **v**, then $\mathbf{x}(t) = e^{\lambda t}\mathbf{v}$ will be a complex solution to the differential equation. It follows from the fact that complex solutions come in conjugate pairs that the real and imaginary parts of a complex solution are real solutions. Maple has built-in facilities **Re** and **Im** for extracting real and imaginary parts of complex numbers.

Find the eigenvectors of the matrix.

```
B := matrix(3 ,3, [1, 2, -1,
                   0, 1, 1,
                   0, -1, 1]);
eigsB := eigenvects(B);
```

When you enter the previous statements, you get the following output. Note that the order of the eigenvalues may be different each time you enter the equations.

```
        [1      2      -1]
        [              ]
B  :=   [0      1      1]
        [              ]
        [0     -1      1]
eigsB := [1, 1, [1, 0, 0]],
         [1 + I, 1, [-1 - 2 I, 1, I]],
         [1 - I, 1, [-1 + 2 I, 1, -I]]
```

The order of the terms of the output in the previous statements is important in what follows. In particular, the first eigenvalue given is real. This gives us one real solution. The second and third eigenvalues are complex, and either one of those leads to a single complex solution for which you can get two real solutions by taking the real and imaginary parts.

Construct a solution from the real eigenvalue.

```
sol1 := exp(eigsB[1][1]*t)*eigsB[1][3][1];
comsol := exp(eigsB[2][1]*t)*eigsB[2][3][1];
sol2 := Re(comsol);
sol3 := Im(comsol);
```

sol2 and **sol3** do not look like real-valued functions because Maple does not automatically distribute multiplication over the vectors and does not simplify complex numbers automatically. You can rectify this using **evalc** after applying **evalm**, which distributes the multiplication and puts the solutions into a nice vector form.

*Construct the general solution and use **evalm** and **evalc** to evaluate the answer.*

```
solB := map(evalc, evalm(C1*sol1 +
   C2*sol2 + C3*sol3));
```

The general vector-valued solution to the differential equation is returned.

If the dimension of each λ-eigenspace is equal to the multiplicity of λ as a root of the characteristic polynomial, we still get n solutions of the form $\mathbf{x}(t) = e^{\lambda t}\mathbf{v}$. This happens when the dimension of the λ-eigenspace is equal to the multiplicity of λ as a root of the characteristic polynomial for each eigenvalue.

If the dimension of one or more of the eigenspaces is less than the multiplicity of the eigenvalue as a root of the characteristic polynomial, there will not exist n linearly independent solutions of the form you are looking for. A general approach to this situation is to look for solutions of the form $\mathbf{x}(t) = e^{\mathbf{A}t}\mathbf{v}$, where $\mathbf{v}$ is a constant vector and $e^{\mathbf{A}t}\mathbf{v}$ is defined as follows:

$$e^{\mathbf{A}t} = \mathbf{I} + \mathbf{A}t + \mathbf{A}^2\frac{t^2}{2!} + \cdots + \mathbf{A}^n\frac{t^n}{n!} + \cdots$$

This infinite series always converges, although in general it is difficult to calculate. Because it converges, the series can be differentiated term by term and, after some simplification, you get

$$\frac{d}{dt}(e^{\mathbf{A}t}\mathbf{v}) = \mathbf{A}e^{\mathbf{A}t}\mathbf{v}$$

It then follows that $e^{\mathbf{A}t}\mathbf{v}$ is a solution of equation (1) for every constant vector $\mathbf{v}$. The general solution will be sums of terms of the form

$$e^{\lambda t}\left(\mathbf{v}_1 + t\mathbf{v}_2 + t^2\mathbf{v}_3 + \cdots + t^{n-1}\mathbf{v}_n\right)$$

where n is the multiplicity of λ as a root of the characteristic polynomial and $\mathbf{v}^1, \ldots, \mathbf{v}^n$ are constant vectors.

Computing $e^{\mathbf{A}t}$ when the eigenvalues of $\mathbf{A}$ can be found.

It turns out that n linearly independent vectors $\mathbf{v}$ can be found for which the infinite series $e^{\mathbf{A}t}\mathbf{v}$ can be summed exactly if the eigenvalues of $\mathbf{A}$ can be computed. We will not explore this fact here, and, in fact, it is beyond the scope of most introductory differential equation texts. It depends on the Cayley-Hamilton theorem, which was introduced in Chapter 4.

Where Maple returns the eigenvalues in the **RootOf** form, you must use **allvalues** to see whether it can find the eigenvalues exactly. Where it cannot, it will return decimal approximations. Making use of approximate solutions obtained from approximated eigenvalues is the subject matter of an entire course and will not be covered here.

Maple has a built-in facility for finding $e^{\mathbf{A}t}$.

If the eigenvalues of a matrix can be found exactly, then $e^{\mathbf{A}t}$ can be calculated. You can then use $e^{\mathbf{A}t}$ to construct the general solution. For many matrices, $\mathbf{A}$, Maple can perform this computation. **dsolve** will not work for some of these examples (at least not in a reasonable amount of time) because it uses more general algorithms, which work on nonlinear equations and may not be efficient for homogeneous linear systems. The Maple command is **exponential** and takes two arguments, a matrix and a variable.

Consider an example where eigenspaces are not sufficient to find all solutions.

```
C := matrix(3, 3, [1, 1, 0,
                   0, 1, 0,
                   0, 0, 2]);
expCt := exponential(C,t);
solC := evalm(C1 * (expCt &* [1, 0, 0]) +
              C2 * (expCt &* [0, 1, 0]) +
              C3 * (expCt &* [0, 0, 1]));
```

Notice that the answer contains a factor of t, as we expect when there are not enough eigenvectors to form a solution that contains only exponentials.

Additional Activities

1. For matrices a–e, find the eigenvalues and eigenvectors, and use these to find the general solution to $\mathbf{x}'(t) = \mathbf{A}\mathbf{x}(t)$ where possible. In other cases, use $e^{\mathbf{A}t}$ to construct the general solution. In each case, where possible, compare with the solution returned by **dsolve**.

    a. $\mathbf{A} = \begin{bmatrix} 1 & 0 & 0 \\ 0 & 2 & 0 \\ 0 & 0 & 3 \end{bmatrix}$

    b. $\mathbf{A} = \begin{bmatrix} 3 & 2 & 4 \\ 2 & 0 & 2 \\ 4 & 2 & 3 \end{bmatrix}$

    c. $\mathbf{A} = \begin{bmatrix} 1 & -2 & 1 \\ 0 & -2 & 1 \\ -1 & 3 & 0 \end{bmatrix}$

d. $A = \begin{bmatrix} 1 & 1 & 1 \\ 2 & 1 & -1 \\ -3 & 2 & 4 \end{bmatrix}$

e. $A = \begin{bmatrix} 2 & 0 & -1 & 0 \\ 0 & 2 & 1 & 0 \\ 0 & 0 & 2 & 0 \\ 0 & 0 & -1 & 2 \end{bmatrix}$

2. Convert the system

$$x'' + 2x - y = 0$$
$$y'' + 2y - x = 0$$

into a linear system of four equations by making the substitutions $x_1(t) = x(t)$, $x_2(t) = x'(t)$, $x_3(t) = y(t)$, $x_4(t) = y'(t)$. Find the eigenvalues and eigenvectors of the resulting system and use them to find the general solution to the system. Find a particular solution for which $x(0) = 0$, $x'(0) = 16$, $y(0) = 0$, $y'(0) = 0$. Make a parametric plot of $x(t)$ versus $y(t)$ for this particular solution.

5.8 **dsolve** Options

Laplace Transforms

There are three options for the Maple **dsolve** operator besides the option **explicit**. These are **laplace**, **series**, and **numeric**. Each of these methods is effective on different types of differential equations. The **laplace** option is well suited for equations that have the following form:

$$ay'' + by' + cy = f(t), \quad y(0) = y_0, \quad y'(0) = y_0'$$

The function, $f(t)$, is referred to as the forcing function.

*Use the **laplace** option to solve $y'' + 2y' - y = \sin(t)$.*

```
lapex := (D@@2)(y)(t) + 2*D(y)(t) -
    y(t) = sin(t);
lapexsol:= dsolve(lapex, y(t), laplace);
```

Notice that the answer contains **y(0)** and **D(y)(0)** as constants. If initial conditions for this method are specified, they must be at 0. Solving this equation without the **laplace** option results in a very different looking answer because Maple uses a different algorithm to solve the equation. It is difficult to verify that the solutions are the same, and Maple is not able to simplify the difference of the two answers to 0. However, you can verify that both answers are actually solutions, and the uniqueness theorem applies in this case to prove they are the same.

Compare the solutions with and without the **laplace** *option.*

```
lapex2 := diff(y(t), t, t) + 2*diff(y(t), t)
   - y(t) = sin(t);
init2 := y(0) = 1, D(y)(0) = 1;
sol1 := dsolve({lapex2, init2},
   y(t),laplace);
sol2 := dsolve({lapex2, init2}, y(t));
simplify(rhs(sol1) - rhs(sol2));
simplify(subs(sol1, lapex2));
simplify(subs(sol2,lapex2));
```

Notice that even though the difference of the two solutions did not simplify to zero, they are both solutions because the last two statements returned $\sin(t) = \sin(t)$. They must therefore be equal.

You can compute the Laplace transform and the inverse Laplace transform.

The **laplace** option for **dsolve** is based on computing Laplace transforms. Maple has a procedure in the **inttrans** package for computing Laplace transforms called **laplace**. To use it to solve an equation, follow these steps:

  i. Laplace-transform the entire equation.

  ii. Solve for the Laplace transform of the dependent variable.

  iii. Inverse-Laplace-transform the resulting equation.

   Either before step ii or after step iii you will want to plug in the initial condition.

Solve
$y'' + y' + 3y = \cos(t)$,
$y(0) = 2, y'(0) = -1$
using Laplace transforms.

```
with(inttrans):
eq := diff(y(t), t, t) + diff(y(t), t) +
   3*y(t)=cos(t);
Leq := laplace(eq, t, s);
LY := solve(Leq, laplace(y(t), t, s));
sol := invlaplace(LY, s, t);
subs(y(0) = 2, D(y)(0) = -1, sol);
```

The solution is displayed. You should compare this answer with the answer you get using **dsolve(...,laplace)**.

Heaviside Function   The method of Laplace transforms is especially applicable in cases where the function, $f(t)$, is discontinuous. Many discontinuous functions can be expressed in terms of a simple function known as the Heaviside function, $H(t)$, which is defined as follows:

$$H(t) = \begin{cases} 0 & \text{if } t < 0 \\ 1 & \text{if } t \geq 0 \end{cases}$$

Maple has the function **Heaviside** built into its library. The **laplace** option for **dsolve** will recognize and solve equations involving the Heaviside function. Consider the following example:

$$y'' + 3y' + 2y = \begin{cases} 1 & \text{if } 0 \leq t \leq 1 \\ 0 & \text{if } t > 1 \end{cases}, \quad y(0) = 0, \ y'(0) = 1$$

This can be written in terms of the Heaviside function as follows:

$$y'' + 3y' + 2y = H(t) - H(t-1), \quad y(0) = 0, \ y'(0) = 1$$

Solve this example.

```
hex := (D@@2)(y)(t) + 3*D(y)(t) + 2*y(t) =
   Heaviside(t) - Heaviside(t - 1);
hinit := y(0) = 0, D(y)(0) = 1;
hexsol := dsolve({hex, hinit},y(t),laplace);
```

The answer, as expected, is given in terms of the Heaviside function. The solution is nevertheless a continuous function, as you can see by plotting the solution.

Sketch the solution.

```
plot(rhs(hexsol), t = 0..10);
```

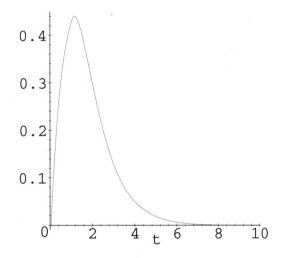

Solution to
$y'' + 3y' + 2y =$
$H(t) - H(t-1),$
$y(0) = 0, \ y'(0) = 1.$

It is common in applications to have more complex discontinuous functions. Consider the function, $g(t)$, given by the graph:

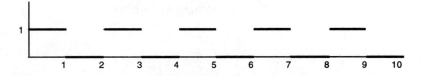

Example of discontinuous function.

This function can be written using the Heaviside function as follows:

$$g(t) = \sum_{n=0}^{n=4} H(t - 2n) - H(t - 2n - 1)$$

You use the **sum** command to express this function and then solve the equation $y'' + 3y + 2y = g(t)$.

Solve this equation and graph the solution.

```
f := sum(Heaviside(t - 2*n) -
        Heaviside(t - 2*n-1), n = 0..4);
eq := (D@@2)(y)(t) + 3*D(y)(t) + 2*y(t) = f;
eqi := y(0) = 0, D(y)(0) = 1;
eqsol := dsolve({eq, eqi}, y(t), laplace);
plot(rhs(eqsol), t = 0..10);
```

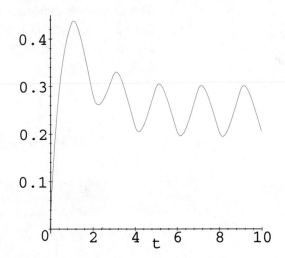

Solution to
$y'' + 3y' + 2y = g(t),$
$y(0) = 0,\ y'(0) = 1.$

Again you see that the solution appears to be continuous.

Additional Activities

1. Use **dsolve** with the **laplace** option to solve each of the initial value problems a–d. Plot the solutions for the interval $0 \le t \le 10$.

a. $y'' + y = \begin{cases} 0, & 0 \le t \le \pi \\ 1, & \pi < t \end{cases}$; $y(0) = 0, \; y'(0) = 1$

b. $y'' + 2y' + y = \begin{cases} t, & 0 \le t \le 1 \\ 0, & 1 < t \end{cases}$; $y(0) = -1, y'(0) = 1$

c. $y'' + y' + 7y = \begin{cases} t, & 0 \le t \le 2 \\ 0, & 2 < t \end{cases}$; $y(0) = 0, y'(0) = 0$

d. $y'' + y = \sum_{n=0}^{4} (H(t - 2n\pi) - H(t - (2n + 1)\pi))$,
$y(0) = 0, y'(0) = 0$

2. Maple also recognizes the Dirac delta function as **Dirac**. Type **?Dirac** for more information. The usual mathematical notation is $\delta(t)$.

a. $y'' + y = \sum_{n=0}^{4} \delta(t - 2n\pi), y(0) = 0, y'(0) = 0$

b. $y'' + y = \sum_{n=0}^{8} \delta(t - n\pi), y(0) = 0, y'(0) = 0$

Series Solutions

Next we will consider general linear differential equations of the form

$$a(t)y''(t) + b(t)y'(t) + c(t)y(t) = f(t)$$

Series solutions offer a way to handle some of these equations. If $a(t)$, $b(t)$, $c(t)$, and $f(t)$ have convergent power series in some interval around a point t_0, then you might expect that the solution has a convergent power series on some interval around t_0.

If $a(t_0) \ne 0$ and $a(t)$, $b(t)$, $c(t)$, and $f(t)$ can be expressed as power series around t_0, then t_0 is called an ordinary point of the differential equation. In this situation, a power series convergent on some interval containing t_0 is given by the Taylor polynomial:

$$y(t) = \sum_{n=0}^{\infty} y^{(n)}(t_0) \frac{(t - t_0)^n}{n!}$$

To find the terms in this power series, calculate the derivatives of y at t_0. Consider the following equation:

$$(1 - t^2)y'' - 6ty' - 4y = 0, \; y(0) = 0, \; y'(0) = 1$$

Look for the first few terms of a series solution near the ordinary point $t = 0$. You find $y''(0)$ by solving the equation for $y''(t)$ and then substituting the value $t = 0$ into the equation.

Find $y''(0)$.

```
sereq := (1 - t^2)*diff(y(t), t, t) -
   2*t*diff(y(t), t) + 4*y(t) = 0;
yppt := solve(sereq,diff(y(t), t, t));
ypp0 := subs({t = 0, y(t) = 0, diff(y(t), t)
   = 1}, yppt);
```

The second derivative in terms of $y(t)$ and $y'(t)$ is displayed and the value of the second derivative at $t = 0$ is displayed. You can then find $y^{(3)}(0)$ by differentiating the equation and then plugging in the initial conditions along with the value you just found for $y''(0)$.

Find $y^{(3)}(0)$.

```
yppp0 := subs({t=0, y(t) = 0,diff(y(t), t)
   = 1, diff(y(t),t,t)=ypp0},diff(yppt, t));
```

The value of the third derivative at $t = 0$ is displayed. To continue this process and calculate $y^{(n)}(0)$ for more terms, it would be best to store the values as you calculate them in a sequence and write a **for** loop to do the calculations. To do any calculations with the resulting solution, you would also have to use these coefficients to form a power series in t. However, Maple will perform all these calculations for you using the **series** option for **dsolve**.

*Use **dsolve** to calculate a series solution.*

```
sereq := (1 - t^2)*diff(y(t), t, t) -
   2*t*diff(y(t), t) + 4*y(t) = 0;
sereqsol := dsolve({sereq, y(0) = 0,
   D(y)(0) = 1}, y(t), series);
```

A fifth-degree polynomial is returned. The order of the series solution returned by the **series** option of **dsolve** is determined by the global variable, **Order**, which is set to 6 by default. If you want more terms, you can change the value of **Order** before calling **dsolve**.

Calculate the tenth-order series solution.

```
Order := 10;
sereq := (1 - t^2)*diff(y(t), t, t) -
   2*t*diff(y(t), t) + 4*y(t) = 0;
sereqsol2 := dsolve({sereq, y(0) = 0,
   D(y)(0) = 1}, y(t), series);
```

Now a ninth-degree polynomial is returned. To extract information from the series solution, such as evaluation at a point or generation of a plot, you must first convert it to a polynomial. Note that the coefficient of $y''(t)$ in this example is equal to 0 at 1 and -1, and thus you expect the solution to be useful only in the range $-1 < t < 1$.

Comparing series solutions of different order using **plot**.

```
poly1 := convert(rhs(sereqsol), polynom);
poly2 := convert(rhs(sereqsol2), polynom);
plot({poly1, poly2}, t = -2..2, -5..5);
```

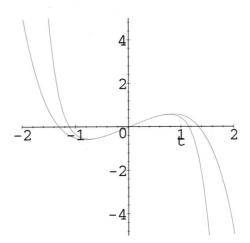

A plot comparing series solutions of different orders.

Recurrence Relations The method of computing derivatives to calculate the terms of a Taylor series has a couple of serious drawbacks. One is that, even with Maple, computing derivatives can be time consuming. The other is that it is difficult to find an expression for the general term of the power series. For example, the kth-order term of the Taylor series for the solution of $y' = y$, $y(0) = 1$ is $x^k/k!$. This can easily be verified using the preceding procedure. However, it is not easy to do this for most equations.

The method of undetermined coefficients.

For an ordinary point, the method of undetermined coefficients does not require calculating any derivatives, but it is assumed that $a(t)$, $b(t)$, and $c(t)$ are given by polynomials in t and that $f(t) = 0$. These conditions are somewhat stronger than is necessary to apply the method. You begin by assuming there is a solution of the form

$$y(t) = \sum_{n=0}^{\infty} a_n t^n$$

where a_0 and a_1 are arbitrary. Substituting this expression into the equation

$$a(t)y''(t) + b(t)y'(t) + c(t)y(t) = 0$$

leads to conditions the coefficients a_n must satisfy. Consider the following example:

$$y'' + t^2y = 0$$

The key to finding the coefficients a_n is that for a power series to vanish identically over any interval, each coefficient in the series must be 0. Thus, after plugging in the power series for $y(t)$, all the coefficients of t on the left-hand side of the resulting equation must be 0 because the right-hand side, $f(t)$, is 0. You can derive the following relation for this equation:

$$\sum_{n=0}^{\infty} n(n-1)a_nt^{n-2} - \sum_{n=0}^{\infty}(n^2 + 5n + 4)a_nt^n = 0$$

By carefully extracting the coefficient of t^k and setting it equal to 0, the following relation for the coefficients is obtained:

$$a_{k+2} = -\frac{1}{(k+2)(k+1)}a_{k-2}$$

This is known as a recurrence relation. Note that to get the kth term you must do all of the sums to $k+2$ because differentiating twice reduces the order of k in the first sum by 2. You sum from $k-2$ because the polynomial coefficients have order ≤ 2, thus increasing the order of k by 2. To see an explanation for **coeff**, type **?coeff** at the Maple prompt.

Find recurrence relation for the a(n).

```
sereq3 := diff(y(t), t, t) + t^2*y(t) = 0;
soly := sum(a[n]*t^n, n = k-2..k+2);
subs(y(t) = soly, sereq3);
termk := coeff(lhs(simplify(")), t^k);
solve(termk, a[k+2]);
```

The output of the last statement is

$$-\frac{a_{k-2}}{2 + k^2 + 3k}$$

The recurrence relation leads to a series solution.

You can write a procedure to calculate $a(n)$ and construct a series approximation to the solution using the recurrence relation. By inspection of the output from the final statement in the previous calculation, you can see that $a[-1]$ and $a[-2]$ are needed in the calculation of $a[2]$ and $a[3]$. Note that $a_0 = y(0)$ and $a_1 = y'(0)$.

Construct the first 10 terms of the series using the recurrence relation.

```
a[-2]  :=  0;
a[-1]  :=  0;
a[0]  :=  a0;
a[1]  :=  a1;
for k from 0 to 7 do
   a[k+2]  :=  -a[k-2]/((k+2)*(k+1))
od;
k  :=  'k';
sereq3sol  :=  sum(a[k]*t^k,  k = 0..9);
```

The ninth-degree polynomial solution is displayed. Compare this answer with the output of the command **dsolve(...,series)** on this example.

Bessel Equations

Equations with singular points.

Series techniques exist to handle the case where t_0 is not an ordinary point for an equation but, in general, the resulting series are not Taylor series. Instead, they involve fractional exponents and logarithm terms. In addition, some solutions will not be defined at the point t_0, and, in particular, you cannot usually specify initial conditions at t_0. Maple will generate series solutions to many of these examples. An example that arises in applications is the following equation, known as Bessel's equation:

$$t^2 y'' + ty' + (t^2 - \mu^2)y = 0$$

where $\mu \geq 0$ is a parameter.

Find a series solution to Bessel's equation with $\mu = 1/2$.

```
besseq  :=  t^2*diff(y(t), t, t) +
   t*diff(y(t),t)+(t^2 - (1/2)^2)*y(t)=0;
besseqsol:= dsolve({besseq}, y(t), series);
```

The series solutions to Bessel's equation have a long history, and a fundamental set of solutions found by techniques beyond what can be discussed here are known as the *Bessel function of the first kind of order* μ, $J_\mu(t)$ and the *Bessel function of the second kind of order* μ, $Y_\mu(t)$. These functions are built into Maple and are returned by the **dsolve** operator when the general Bessel equation is entered.

*Use **dsolve** to solve Bessel's equation.*

```
besseqmu := t^2*diff(y(t), t, t)+
    t*diff(y(t),t) + (t^2-(mu)^2)*y(t)=0;
besseqsol := dsolve({besseqmu}, y(t));
```

The solution is returned in terms of the built-in Maple functions **BesselJ** and **BesselY**.

Additional Activities

1. Using paper and pencil, find the recurrence relationship for

$$y' - y = 0$$

centered at $t = 0$.

   Following the outline of this section, use Maple to find the recurrence relationship. Because it is a first-order equation, you should solve the kth term for $a[k + 1]$. Does your result agree with the Taylor series of the known solution $y(t) = y(0)e^t$?

2. Find the series solution centered at $t = 0$ for the equation

$$(1 - t^2)y'' - 6ty - 4y = 0$$

   Find the recurrence relationship for the coefficients and compare the resulting series solution with the first 10 terms obtained using **dsolve, series**.

3. Find the series solution centered at $t = 0$ for the equation

$$y' + 3t^5 y = 0$$

   To find the recurrence relationship using Maple, sum from $k - 5$ to $k + 1$. Because it is a first-order equation, solve the kth term for $a[k + 1]$. Set $a[n] = 0$ for the appropriate number of negative values n when constructing the Taylor series from the recurrence relationship. Compare with the result of **dsolve, series** for the first 10 terms.

4. Find the series solution centered at $t = 1$ for the equation

$$y'' + ty' + 2y - t - 3 = 0, \quad y(1) = 0, \quad y'(1) = 1$$

First, make the substitution $t = z + 1$ and solve the equation

$$\frac{d^2y}{dz^2} + (1 + z)\frac{dy}{dz} + 2y - 4 - z = 0$$

centered at $z = 0$. Then, substitute $z = t - 1$ into the resulting Taylor series.

Index